D0848467

Polygamy
The Mormon Enigma

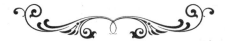

E. Keith Howick

Books by E. Keith Howick

The Life of Jesus the Messiah Series

The Miracles of Jesus the Messiah
The Parables of Jesus the Messiah
The Sermons of Jesus the Messiah
The Mission of Jesus the Messiah
The Second Coming of Jesus the Messiah*
*Notable Book Award, 2004 Writers Notes Book Awards

The Challenged by the Restoration Series

Challenged by the Old Testament
Challenged by the New Testament
Challenged by The Book of Mormon
Challenged by The Doctrine and Covenants
Challenged by Church History

A Concise History of the Early Church Series

A Concise History of Palmyra
A Concise History of Kirtland
A Concise History of Zion
A Concise History of Nauvoo

Other Books

Prophets of the Old Testament

The *Index* to the *History of the Church of Jesus Christ of Latter-day Saints*

Polygamy
The Mormon Enigma

E. Keith Howick

WindRiver Publishing
SILVERTON, IDAHO

Queries, comments or correspondence concerning this work should be directed to the author and submitted to WindRiver Publishing at Authors@WindRiverPublishing.com.

http://www.WindRiverPublishing.com

Polygamy: The Mormon Enigma

Copyright ©2007 by E. Keith Howick

Front cover quotation from a speech delivered by Mitt Romney at the St. Patrick's Day Breakfast, Boston, 2005. Quoted in *Newsweek,* March 26, 2007.

Front cover photograph of the LDS Temple ©2006 Ricardo630/CC Attribution ShareAlike 2.5.

WindRiver Publishing, the WindRiver Brand Logo, and the WindRiver Windmill Logo are trademarks of WindRiver Publishing, Inc., 72 N WindRiver Road, Silverton, ID 83867-0446.

Library of Congress Control Number: 2007939882
ISBN-13 978-1-886249-19-6
ISBN-10 1-886249-19-9

First Printing 2007
Printed in the U.S.A. by Malloy, Inc., on acid-free paper

Contents

Enigma (noun)

Pronounced *i-'nig-me*

Etymology: Latin *aenigma,* from Greek *ainig-mat-, ainigma,* from *ainissesthai* to speak in riddles, from *ainos* fable.

1. A perplexing, baffling, or seemingly inexplicable matter or thing.

2. Something that is not easily or satisfactorily explained or understood.

3. Mysterious or puzzling.

Abbreviations _____

The following abbreviations are used in footnotes throughout the book. For a complete list of sources cited including complete citations see the Bibliography.

A&B Leonard J. Arrington and Davis Bitton, *The Mormon Experience: A History of the Latter-day Saints.*

D. Johnson Donald Bruce Johnson (ed), *National Party Platforms: Volume I 1840–1856.*

J. Johnson Jeffrey O. Johnson, "Determining and Defining 'Wife': The Brigham Young Households," *Dialogue: A Journal of Mormon Thought.*

Bachman Daniel W. Bachman, "A Study of the Mormon Practice of Plural Marriage before the Death of Joseph Smith."

Campbell Eugene E. Campbell, *Establishing Zion: The Mormon Church in the American West.*

Compton Todd Compton, *In Sacred Loneliness: The Plural Wives of Joseph Smith.*

D&C *The Doctrine and Covenants* of the Church of Jesus Christ of Latter-day Saints.

Ed Alfred Edersheim, *The Life and Times of Jesus the Messiah.*

Embry Jessie L. Embry, *Setting the Record Straight, Mormons & Polygamy.*

HC Joseph Smith, Jr., *History of The Church of Jesus Christ of Latter-day Saints.*

JC James E. Talmage, *Jesus the Christ.*

JD Brigham Young, et al., Journal of Discourses.

Larson Gustave O. Larson, *The "Americanization" of Utah for Statehood.*

RHC *History of the Church of Jesus Christ of Latter Day Saints,* Board of Publication of the Reorganized Church of Jesus Christ of Latter Day Saints.

Richardson James D. Richardson, *A Compilation of the Messages and Papers of the Presidents, 1789–1897.*

Roberts B. H. Roberts, *Comprehensive History of the Church of Jesus Christ of Latter-day Saints.*

Shin Ian Shin, "'Scoot–Smoot–Scoot': The Seating Trial of Senator Reed Smoot," *Gains Junction Undergraduate Interdisciplinary Journal of History.*

Smith Joseph Fielding Smith, *Blood Atonement and the Origin of Plural Marriage.*

Statutes *By Authority of Congress: the Statutes at Large of the United States of America.*

Trench Richard C. Trench, *Notes on the Parables of Our Lord.*

Young Kimball Young, *Isn't One Wife Enough?*

Zion Edwin Brown Firmage and Richard Collin Mangrum, *Zion In The Courts: A Legal History of the Church of Jesus Christ of Latter-day Saints 1830–1900.*

Foreword _____

It is obvious that former Massachusetts Governor Mitt Romney's candidacy for the Presidency of the United States has once again made the issue of polygamy front page news. Does it matter? *Should* it matter? In a nation that goes out of its way to separate church and state, wouldn't it be logical to assume that the American public would separate a candidate's religious beliefs from his or her political qualifications?

At this writing, Mr. Romney, an active member of the Church of Jesus Christ of Latter-day Saints (aka the LDS Church or the "Mormons") is in the top tier of the Republican candidates running in the 2008 presidential race. In interviews, he is frequently asked about his religion and about polygamy. These are hot-button issues, and have been ever since the early Mormon practice of polygamy was initiated by the Prophet Joseph Smith[1] in the early 1830s.

In the 1856 presidential race, the initiative to

---

[1] Members of the Church of Jesus Christ of Latter-day Saints commonly refer to Joseph Smith as a "prophet," or the "Prophet." That terminology is used in places throughout this text.

eradicate the "twin relics of barbarism: polygamy and slavery,"[2] was couched in the Republican Party platform.[3] Between the years of 1852 and 1890, the topic of polygamy was overshadowed by opposition to slavery and the resulting Civil War. After the Civil War, Congress spent the next twenty-five years working intently to destroy both polygamy and the Mormon Church.[4]

After issuing the Manifesto in 1890 and what has been termed the "second" Manifesto in 1904,[5] the LDS Church officially stopped the practice of polygamy. However, it continued to be a political issue. In 1896, the United States Government required Utah to permanently ban polygamy in its Constitution before it would grant the territory statehood and in 1899, when Mormon Church leader Brigham H. Roberts was elected to Congress as the Representative from the State of Utah, the House of Representatives refused to seat him because he still practiced and believed in polygamy.

When Mormon Apostle Reed Smoot won the Utah Senatorial race in 1903, the Committee on Privileges and Elections initiated a trial to prohibit his seating—even though he was not a polygamist. Although he was temporarily seated while his tri-

---

[2] *Congressional Globe* (Washington, D.C.; Government Printing Office, 1860), 1410.

[3] Donald B. Johnson, *National Party Platforms: Volume I,* 1840–1956 (Champaign: University of Illinois Press, 1966), 27–28.

[4] The Manifesto of 1890 is currently published at the end of *The Doctrine and Covenants* as "Official Declaration—1."

[5] See Chapter 7.

al proceeded, it took the power of the President and other powerful political figures to overcome a four-year debate and the 3,482 vitriolic petitions the committee received denouncing Mr. Smoot, polygamy, and the Mormon Church. (The committee voted 7 to 5 to prohibit seating, but when the Senate voted, it reversed the committee's decision and voted 42 to 28 in favor of officially seating Mr. Smoot as a United States Senator.)

Two world wars and the great depression delayed any further anti-polygamy activity until the 1940s and 1950s when government officials from Utah and Arizona initiated raids on Short Creek, Arizona (now Colorado City, Arizona, and Hildale, Utah). They arrested and tried polygamist husbands under the anti-bigamy and illegal cohabitation acts of those states. (Although these groups claimed *The Book of Mormon* and the teachings of Joseph Smith as the foundation of their religious beliefs, none of them were associated with the Church of Jesus Christ of Latter-day Saints.)

Intermittent anti-polygamy activity took place during the next fifty years[6] until on August 30, 2006, Warren Jeffs, a non-Mormon polygamist leader who had been on the FBI's "Ten Most Wanted" list, was arrested in Nevada. He was convicted of being an accomplice to rape and as of November 2007, his case is still on appeal.

---

[6] See Appendix C for a time line of polygamist activities between the 1830s and 2007.

As of 2007, many state constitutions specifically prohibit polygamy.[7] However, law enforcement agencies in two of these states—Utah and Arizona—have decided to primarily focus on crimes within polygamous communities that involve child abuse, domestic violence, welfare fraud, and "child polygamy,"[8] rather than polygamy itself. The Attorneys General in Utah and Arizona have worked together to produce a manual entitled, *The Primer: Helping Victims of Domestic Violence and Child Abuse in Polygamous Communities.* This manual provides basic information about various polygamous communities that can assist human services professionals, law enforcement officers, and others in helping victims from these societies.

On May 13, 2007, Mitt Romney (who has polygamist ancestors) appeared on CBS' *60 Minutes* and described the Mormon doctrine of polygamy as "awful." This oxymoron raises the question, how much do people really know about the practice of polygamy in the Mormon Church? Should it be considered a political issue, or merely an historical religious practice?

The American people will always decide for themselves what is and what is not important during a presidential race; this is something candidates can

---

[7] Arizona Constitution, Article XX, Paragraph 2; Idaho Constitution, Article I, Paragraph 4; New Mexico Constitution, Article XXI, Paragraph 1; Oklahoma Constitution, Article I, Paragraph 2; Utah Constitution, Article III.

[8] Child polygamy laws passed in 2003 and 2005 by Utah and Arizona increase the legal marriageable age of a girl from 14 to 18.

influence but cannot control. It is obvious at this point, however, that during the upcoming election, Mormon polygamy will remain the controversial enigma it has been for more than 170 years.

Introduction _____

Early members of the LDS faith chose to embrace the practice of polygamy for spiritual reasons, but the perception of polygamy to outsiders and antagonists of the church was quite different. Anti-Mormons considered polygamy to be immoral, lustful, and womanizing, and decried it as "spiritual wifery." Others envisioned licentious situations such as harems where the "lord and master" floated from flower to flower sating his sexual appetite with a plethora of beautiful wives. In modern times, many think of polygamy in terms of men secretly having families in different cities and attempting to be a husband and/or father to each family without the others finding out about it. Many television shows have effectively used this provocative storyline in their programming. The most recent use of polygamy in mainstream entertainment is in HBO's drama/comedy, "Big Love," which (unlike previous entries in the media) uses polygamy as its primary storyline.

But for Mormons, all of these scenarios depict

something that is far from the truth. To faithful members, polygamy is part of a commandment from God that is encapsulated within Section 132 of *The Doctrine and Covenants,* one of the standard works[1] of the Church of Jesus Christ of Latter-day Saints. It was not widely practiced at first, but since records are sketchy from that period, it is impossible to determine an accurate count of those who were actually called to live the law.

B.H. Roberts in his *Comprehensive History of the Church* states that only 2 percent of LDS men in the early church were polygamists.[2] Joseph Fielding Smith agreed with that figure in his *Essentials in Church History.* Most researchers consider that figure too low, however.[3] Today, a figure of between 10 and 20 percent is usually considered accurate. This means, of course, that at least *80 percent of the early Mormons were monogamous.*[4]

Even the church's founding prophet, Joseph Smith, was reluctant to take additional wives. On several occasions he told people that an angel (with sword in hand) had appeared to him multiple times and told him that if he did not obey the principle, he would be slain.[5] Overall, it is estimated that as

---

[1] The Standard Works of the Church of Jesus Christ of Latter-day Saints comprise the *Bible, The Book of Mormon, The Doctrine and Covenants,* and *The Pearl of Great Price.*

[2] Roberts 1930, 6:149.

[3] Embry 2007, 72.

[4] A&B 1979, 199.

[5] Smith n/d, 67–68.

few as twenty-nine men were called to enter into polygamous marriages during the Joseph Smith period.[6] Those who attempted to practice polygamy on their own or to use it for lustful purposes were either rebuked or excommunicated.[7]

So what was it like in those days to live in a polygamous relationship? As with any monogamous relationship, it differed from family to family. Some families succeeded and some failed. Some were happy, some were not. They were influenced by the same issues that affect us today: finances, health, age, living conditions, education, intellect, and religious commitment. "After all, the plural family was really but an appendage to the basic patriarchal monogamous family. In matters such as the location of the families—whether under the same roof all together or in separate households in the same community or in different localities—there were no definite rules."[8]

Divorce was possible in polygamous relationships. One study reported that Brigham Young granted 1,645 divorces during his tenure as Prophet and leader of the church, including some of his own.[9] Although many of those divorces were handled through the courts, some were obtained in a more casual manner. Mary Woodward, who

---

[6] Embry 2007, 33.

[7] HC 1955, 5:18.

[8] Young 1954, 153–154.

[9] Embry 2007, 82.

had been married to Brigham less than a year, asked to be "released" or divorced from him by letter. Brigham merely wrote back stating, "you may [consider] yourself discharged from me and my counsel," and she was free of the relationship. Another of Brigham's wives, Mary Ann Clark Powers, asked to be released from "all engagements with [Brigham] for time and eternity." Brigham merely agreed.

The most famous of Brigham's divorces was from Ann Eliza Webb Young, his twenty-seventh wife. She pursued divorce through the courts, even though the marriage had not been recorded civilly. The court ordered Brigham to pay her $500 a month for an allowance and $3,000 in court costs. Brigham refused, and was fined $25.00 and one day in jail—which he served.[10] Ann Eliza was later excommunicated and from 1875 on, spent much of her life speaking and writing about polygamy.[11]

Many theories have been postulated concerning why the early members of the LDS Church wanted to enter into polygamous relationships. However, it is quite evident that Joseph (and those who followed him) considered it a sacred duty. They felt compelled to comply with the requirements of the Lord's revelation (not to mention the fact that they were threatened with spiritual damnation if they

[10] Embry 2007, 35.

[11] J. Johnson 1987, 62–63.

did not).[12] Furthermore, although divorces were occasionally granted, most women remained in their polygamous relationships because they had received a spiritual confirmation that the principle was true.[13]

You can go to your local bookstore or online and find dozens of stories about Mormon men and women who practiced polygamy between the early 1830s and 1904. Some accounts present the lifestyle in a positive light, others are negative. Some are factual; some are not. It is often difficult to separate the wheat from the chaff in these narratives due to the authors' perspectives. On the one hand we have authors who fervently believe the Lord commanded early church members to live in polygamy and that they were being righteous to do so. On the other hand, there are those who just as fervently believe that any polygamous relationship is wrong, even evil. This book will answer many questions about polygamy, but perhaps one of the most crucial questions is why? Why is there such a strong dichotomy of opinion on the subject of polygamy?

---

[12] D&C 1981, 132:3–4.

[13] Bachman 1975, 493.

Chapter One _____

Polygamy Facts

History has provided us with the following facts:

- Joseph Smith and others practiced polygamy starting in the early 1830s, long before the doctrine was publicly acknowledged by Brigham Young in 1852.

- Polygamy was initially practiced in secret, limiting the number of church members who knew about the revelation and who adhered to it.

- The Church of Jesus Christ of Latter-day Saints, also called "Mormons," practiced polygamy before (and to a limited degree after) the Manifesto of 1890.[1]

- From its inception, the practice was illegal under the laws of the states in which the members of the LDS Church lived.[2] Additionally, after

[1] In the Manifesto of 1890, President Wilford Woodruff announced that Congress had enacted laws which forbade plural marriages and declared his intention to submit to those laws, and to use his influence to have church members do the same.

[2] Various people in the western European cultures had been practicing bigamy and polygamy for hundreds of years before the creation of the LDS church, although not in a religious context. The Commonwealth of England had anti-bigamy laws long before the United States became a nation, and the United States adopted those laws as a matter of course.

Utah[3] became an official territory, the federal government passed laws outlawing the practice of polygamy in all U.S. territories. Polygamy and bigamy were also against the law in both Mexico[4] and Canada during the time they were practiced by the church in those countries.

- The practice of (and belief in) the doctrine of polygamy was, from time to time, publicly denied during the administration of Joseph Smith. Brigham Young finally ordered a public acknowledgment of the practice in 1852.

- The LDS Church fought the legal system that criminalized the practice of polygamy until late in the nineteenth century, but the Supreme Court of the United States declared those laws *constitutional.*

- The laws passed by Congress during the anti-polygamy period (1862–1890) were instigated by both public hysteria and religious persecution of the Mormons. Today, such laws would, in all probability, be declared unconstitutional as a "bill of attainder" (a legislative act that singles out an individual or group for punishment without a trial).[5]

---

[3] Utah was originally called the Territory or State of Deseret.

[4] William Alexander Linn, *The Story Of The Mormons From The Date Of Origin To The Year 1901* (New York: The MacMillan Company; London: Macmillan & Co., Ltd., 1902), 614.

[5] U.S. Constitution, Article 1, Section 9, Paragraph 3.

- During the late 1800s and early 1900s, the government of the United States attempted to destroy not only the practice of polygamy, but the LDS Church itself.

The critics of the LDS Church, both past and present, have always assailed the practice of polygamy. They have been particularly critical of the fact that Joseph Smith and other early Saints denied having multiple wives. In a discussion with Lorenzo Snow in Nauvoo, Joseph disclosed the fact that he had foreseen the problems the church would encounter once the commandment to live the law of plural wives was made public. It appears he knew the storm was coming.[6]

It is not possible today to determine exactly why the early brethren denied having more than one wife—no written explanation has been found. Although several plausible reasons for their denials will be discussed in Chapter Four, fear was undoubtedly one of the major factors. From the inception of the church, Smith and his followers had been under continuous persecution, not only because they were "Mormons" and believed in visions and revelation, but because they believed in a unique book that had been translated from gold plates.[7]

The enemies of the church used every possible

---

[6] See Chapter Three.

[7] The term "Mormons" was originally used derogatorily to label members of the LDS Church.

8

excuse to justify the hatred and abuse they heaped upon early church members. During the Missouri period of church history, Lilburn W. Boggs, the Governor of Missouri during that period, went so far as to issue an Extermination Order against the Saints.[8] If the doctrine of polygamy had been openly promoted at that time, persecution would undoubtedly have intensified to the point that the church may have been destroyed. And so the LDS leaders' denials, in one form or another, may have been merely a means of self-preservation.

Early LDS Church leaders may have found support for their denials in the Bible. There are at least two stories in the Old Testament and several involving Paul in the New Testament that relate historical incidents where the Lord allowed His followers to conceal the truth in order to preserve their lives or further His work. In the Old Testament, both Abraham and Isaac gave potentially dangerous rulers false information about their wives; both of these Patriarchs claimed that their wives were actually their sisters. After the truth was revealed, Abraham used the excuse that Sarah actually *was* his sister. They both had the same father but different mothers, which made Sarah his half-sister. But Isaac had no such relationship with Rebekah (although she was the daughter of his uncle, Abraham's brother, which made her his

---

[8] See HC 1955, 3:175 for the full order by Governor Lilburn W. Boggs to either "exterminate" the Mormons or "drive them from the state."

cousin). Why did they conceal the truth? Fear! Both of these prophets told their wives to partic- ipate in the deceptions because otherwise, they feared they would be killed. The result was that they were asked to leave the countries they were in, but they were not harmed.[9]

In the New Testament, a man named Saul went about severely persecuting the members of Christ's church. However, once he was converted to Christ (at which point his name was changed to Paul) and was actively promulgating the gospel, he was not opposed to using his past affiliation with the Jews to his advantage, both while proselyting and while protecting himself from the Jews' vengeance. He declared frankly to the Corinthians:

> And unto the Jews I became as a Jew, that I might gain the Jews; to them that are un- der the law, as under the law, that I might gain them that are under the law;
>
> To them that are without law, as with- out law, (being not without law to God, but under the law to Christ), that I might gain them that are without law.
>
> To the weak became I as weak, that I might gain the weak: I am made all things to all men, that I might by all means save some.
>
> And this I do for the gospel's sake, that I might be partaker thereof with you.[10]

---

[9] See Genesis 12:13–20; 20:2–17; 26:7–11.

[10] 1 Corinthians 9:20–23.

Paul undoubtedly gave this explanation to justify actions that may have seemed inconsistent and deceptive to his fellow Christians. For example, years after his conversion he went into the temple in Jerusalem and purified himself by performing the necessary sacrifices and oblations the Jewish law required, even though he had previously argued that these requirements under the Law of Moses had been replaced by the gospel and were no longer necessary for Gentile converts.[11]

On another occasion, Paul was arrested by the Jews and brought before their council. It was obvious that they had murderous intentions. The council was composed of both Pharisees and Sadducees so Paul, knowing that the Pharisees believed in the resurrection and the Sadducees did not, raised this controversial issue. This resulted in an uproar that directed their attention away from Paul and spared him the necessity of expressing *his* convictions, which saved his life at the time.[12]

In these and other instances in the Bible, circumstances dictated a veiled response that preserved the integrity and sometimes the very lives of certain individuals and allowed them to continue promulgating the word of God, as it apparently did the early Mormon brethren who were practicing polygamy.

---

[11] Acts 21:26.

[12] Acts 23:1–9.

Chapter Two _____

Biblical Polygamy

Many of the revelations Joseph Smith received—including his first vision—came as a result of his questioning mind. During December of 1830, he recorded in his diary that he had already commenced a retranslation of the Bible.[1] It may have been during this period of time that his New England background caused him to question the justification for Old Testament Patriarchs having multiple wives and concubines. Joseph was raised in a monogamous family; he knew no other lifestyle. Therefore, it is reasonable to assume that he would be curious about a system that differed from his own, yet was accepted by God.[2]

The sacred ordinance of marriage was instituted in the Garden of Eden when God created man and woman. After citing the need for the creation of woman, He commanded, "Therefore shall a man leave his father and his mother, and shall cleave unto his wife: and they shall be one flesh."[3] Jesus confirmed this relationship when the

---

[1] HC 1955, 1:132.

[2] D&C 132:1.

[3] Genesis 2:18–24.

the Pharisees questioned Him about divorce. He replied, "Have ye not read, that he which made them at the beginning made them male and female . . . For this cause shall a man leave father and mother, and shall cleave to his wife: and they twain shall be one flesh? Wherefore they are no more twain, but one flesh. What therefore God hath joined together, let not man put asunder."[4] Polygamy, being a form of marriage, would fall under this edict.

The Biblical history of polygamy began early. Lamech, a descendant of Cain (Abel's brother) is the first man recorded as having multiple wives.[5] The next recorded polygamous marriage was that of Abraham,[6] the same Abraham with whom God made His covenant.[7] In any reading of the Old Testament, whether Joseph's retranslation,[8] the King James Bible, or any other translation, it is evident that polygamy was practiced by the ancient patriarchs and continued under the Law of Moses, where rules were made regarding the regulation and privileges of wives and concubines.[9]

---

[4] Matthew 19:3–9.

[5] Genesis 4:19.

[6] Genesis 16:3; 25:6.

[7] Genesis 17:1–2.

[8] Joseph Smith's retranslation of the Bible is now known to members of the LDS Church as the *Joseph Smith Translation.*

[9] Exodus 21:10; Deuteronomy 21:15. Concubines were considered wives of secondary rank, inferior to actual wives. Under the Law of Moses they were protected (Exodus 21:7–8) and regulated, (Exodus 21:7–9) but they were occasionally detached from the normal family unit by the wives. (Genesis 21:14; 25:6.) They had no authority in the family, nor could they share in household government. One example of why concubines were taken by men can be gleaned from the stories of Abraham and Jacob where the first wife could not produce an heir. In the case of Jacob, the situation was fraught with the competition and jealousy that existed between Leah and Rachael. (Genesis 30.)

Some of the men in the Old Testament who lived in polygamous relationships are well known. King Solomon, perhaps the most famous, had one thousand wives and concubines,[10] but there are at least 27 other men specifically identified in the Old Testament who also had multiple wives and/or concubines and some who, because of the number of their children, were probably living with more than one wife.[11] However, while polygamy was a common practice in Biblical times, it was also a common practice in many other cultures.[12]

In the New Testament, the Jews were still living under the Law of Moses and while there are no specific references in the text identifying polygamous relationships, it is generally accepted that the practice continued.[13] Here again, instructions are recorded regarding the duties of a husband and wife[14] and Paul declared that the marriage relation-

---

[10] 1 Kings 11:1–3.

[11] See Appendix A.

[12] Many ancient cultures practiced polygamy. Multiple wives evidenced a man's wealth and prestige. During the days of Genghis Khan, multiple wives were an accepted part of society and played an important role. "Tribal chiefs often sought the opinion and advice of their wives."[a] Polygamy was also practiced in China[b], in India[c], and in many other ancient cultures.

[a] Leo De Hartog, *Genghis Khan: Conqueror of the World* (New York: Barnes & Noble Publishing, 1999), 10.

[b] Fatima Wu, "From a Dead End to a New Road of Life: Xiao Sa's Abandoned Women," *World Literature Today*, 1991, 65.

[c] John Renard, *Responses to 101 Questions on Hinduism* (Mahwah: Paulist Press, March 1999).

[13] Alfred Edersheim, *Sketches of Jewish Social Life in the Days of Christ* (Grand Rapids: Wm. B. Eerdmans Publishing Company, reprinted 1982), 142.

[14] Ephesians 5:22–33; Colossians 3:18–19; 1 Peter 3:1–7.

ship was "honorable,"[15] augmenting the instructions the Lord had given to Adam and Eve. The scriptures make it clear that the Lord was more concerned about the quality of the marriage relationship than he was about how many women with whom a man shared that relationship.

Because of the evidence available showing God justified polygamous relationships in the Bible, it is reasonable to assume that Joseph Smith, who by nature was a curious man, would inquire of the Lord "touching the principle and doctrine of [the Patriarchs] having many wives and concubines."[16] The result, of course, was the revelation on celestial marriage recorded in Section 132 of *The Doctrine and Covenants,* and all that it entailed.

---

[15] Hebrews 13:4.

[16] D&C 132:1.

Chapter Three _____
Mormon Polygamy

Exactly *when* The Church of Jesus Christ of Latter-day Saints incorporated the practice of polygamy into its doctrine is unknown. Some place it as early as 1831, others at a later date; but all agree that by 1842 it was being practiced in Nauvoo, Illinois, and was an accepted doctrine of the church—even though it was not publicly acknowledged and in some instances, was even publicly denied.

On February 16, 1874, William Clayton, clerk to the Prophet Joseph Smith, gave a sworn statement before John T. Caine, a notary public in Salt Lake City, Utah. In that statement he asserted the following:

On the 7th of October, 1842, in the presence of Bishop Newel K. Whitney and his wife, Elizabeth Ann, President Joseph Smith appointed me Temple Recorder, and also his private clerk, placing all records, books, papers, etc., in my care, and requiring me to take charge of and preserve them, his closing words being, "when I have any revelations to write, you are the one to write them."

Then Brother Clayton went on to record this interesting historical event.

On the morning of the 12th of July, 1843, Joseph and his brother, Hyrum Smith, came into the office in the upper story of the brick store, on the bank of the Mississippi river. They were talking on the subject of plural marriage. Hyrum said to Joseph, "If you will write the revelation on celestial marriage [an obvious indication that the revelation had been given and made known prior to this date], I will take it and read it to Emma, and I believe I can convince her of its truth, and you will hereafter have peace." [Emma obviously knew of the revelation prior to this time and had been opposed to it and to Joseph complying with it.] Joseph smiled and remarked, "You do not know Emma as well as I do." Hyrum repeated his opinion, and further remarked, "The doctrine is so plain, I can convince any reasonable man or woman of its truth, purity and heavenly origin," or words to that effect. Joseph then said,

"Well, get paper and prepare to write." Hyrum very urgently requested Joseph to write the revelation by means of the Urim and Thummim, but Joseph in reply, said he did not need to, for he knew the revelation perfectly from beginning to end.

Joseph and Hyrum then sat down and Joseph commenced to dictate the revelation on celestial marriage, and I wrote it, sentence by sentence, as he dictated. After the whole was written, Joseph asked me to read it through, slowly and carefully, which I did, and he pronounced it correct. He then remarked that there was much more that he could write on the same subject, but what was written was sufficient for the present.

Hyrum [who purportedly had at least two wives[1]] then took the revelation to read to Emma. Joseph remained with me in the office until Hyrum returned. When he came back, Joseph asked him how he had succeeded. Hyrum replied that he had never received a more severe talking to in his life, that Emma was very bitter and full of resentment and anger.

Joseph quietly remarked, "I told you you did not know Emma as well as I did."

---

[1] Buchman 1975, 495.

Joseph then put the revelation in his pocket, and they both left the office.[2]

Brother Clayton stated that the revelation was read to several of the "authorities" that day, and in the evening Bishop Newel K. Whitney asked Joseph if he could have a copy. Joseph agreed and a copy was made by Joseph C. Kingsbury. Brother Clayton then recorded this interesting event between Joseph and Emma concerning the original copy of the revelation:

> Two or three days after the revelation was written Joseph related to me and several others that Emma had so teased, and urgently entreated him for the privilege of destroying it, that he became so weary of her teasing, and to get rid of her annoyance, he told her she might destroy it and she had done so, but he had consented to her wish in this matter to pacify her, realizing that he knew the revelation perfectly and could rewrite it at any time if necessary.

A copy of the revelation was preserved by Bishop Whitney, "and few knew of its existence until the temporary location of the Camp of Israel at Winter Quarters, on the Missouri River, in 1846."[3]

---

[2] HC 1955, 5:xxxii–xxxiii.

[3] HC 1955, 5:xxxii–xxxiii. For the complete affidavit, see the *Deseret Evening News*, 20 May 1886.

Joseph C. Kingsbury also gave a notarized statement before Charles W. Stayner, a notary public in Salt Lake City, Utah, that he indeed did make a copy of the revelation, which was compared to the original before it was destroyed by Emma. He also stated that he personally knew that Joseph had married other women besides Emma and identified one of them as Sarah Ann Whitney, the eldest daughter of Bishop Whitney and Elizabeth Ann Whitney.[4]

The revelation spoken of herein deals with the subject of celestial marriage. It first appeared in the 1876 edition of *The Doctrine and Covenants* as Section 132. The heading preceding the revelation notes that the revelation was recorded July 12, 1843; however, there is "indisputable evidence that the revelation making known this marriage law was given to the Prophet as early as 1831."[5]

The following list provides the most convincing evidence that the revelation and practice existed during or prior to 1841:[6]

1. Accusations were made against the church for polygamous marriages in 1835 and 1836.

2. Aaron Lyon was tried by the church in 1838 for claiming to receive a revelation that Sister Jack-

---

[4] HC 1955, 5:xxxiii–xxxiv.

[5] HC 1955, 5:xxix.

[6] HC 1955, 3:26; 5:xxx–xxxi; 5:78–79.

son, "a married woman, and whose husband was still living, was to become his wife."

3. John C. Bennett accused LDS Church leaders of practicing polygamy, as recorded in his book, *The History of the Saints,* published in 1842.

4. Orson Pratt and Lyman Johnson both testified that Joseph had received the revelation as early as 1831, and had wives sealed to him as early as April 5, 1841.

Emma continued to steadfastly deny the allegation that Joseph had other wives, even though she had been taught the principle and had witnessed multiple women sealed to the Prophet.[7] After Joseph's Death, she (along with Joseph Smith III and others of the Reorganized Church of Jesus Christ of Latter Day Saints [RLDS, now known as the "Community of Christ"]) stated that the revelation was a fabrication concocted by Brigham Young to justify the plurality of wives doctrine. They supported this assertion with the fact that the revelation on and the practice of polygamy was not publicly acknowledged until 1852. In addition, Joseph Smith III, who became president of the RLDS Church when it was founded in 1860, constantly denied that his father had anything to do with either the revelation on celestial marriage or polyg-

---

[7] HC 1955, 5:xxxii–xxxiii; see also RHC 1911, Volumes III and IV.

amy. Between 1860 and 1890, members of the RLDS faith made considerable efforts to discredit the revelation. Some of the members even made visits to Utah to preach against polygamy and to challenge LDS Church leaders to public debates on the subject.[8] However, many writers have demonstrated that Joseph Smith had plural wives, which contradicts their position. Daniel Bachman documents a total of 31 wives, George D. Smith lists 43, D. Michael Quinn cites 46, and Fawn Brodie claims Joseph had 48 wives. Todd D. Compton argues that there is well-documented evidence of 33 marriages in addition to Emma, with the earliest being that of Fanny Alger in early 1833. Even the LDS Church's Ancestral File lists 24.

The makeup of the 33 polygamous marriages documented in Todd Compton's book is interesting. According to Compton, the ages of Joseph's 33 wives ranged from 14 to 58. Thirty-three percent were 14–20 years old; 27 percent were 21–30; 24 percent were 31–40; 6 percent were 41–50; and 9 percent were 51–58. It is also interesting to note from Compton's work that Joseph entered into what is known as "polyandry," a polygamous relationship with a woman that is already married and living with her husband.[9] At least eight of the marriages were of this type.

---

[8] RHC 1911, Volumes III and IV. Note: the RLDS Church and the LDS Church both gave the same title to their early history books except in the RLDS editions, the latter part of the title is written "Latter Day Saints," while the LDS Church uses "Latter-day Saints."

[9] Compton 1997, 4–16. See Appendix B for a list of women documented to have been wives of Joseph Smith.

Regarding the everlasting covenant of marriage (specifically the plurality of wives), Joseph stated the following: "These holy and sacred ordinances have nothing to do with whoredoms, unlawful connections, confusion or crime; but the very reverse. They have laws, limits, and bounds of the strictest kind, and none but the pure in heart, the strictly virtuous, or those who repent and become such, are worthy to partake of them. And . . . [a] dreadful weight of condemnation awaits those who pervert, or abuse them."[10]

President Lorenzo Snow stated that upon his return from his European mission in April of 1843, he went to visit the Prophet. They walked down near the Mississippi River in Nauvoo and sat upon a log and talked. In a later affidavit, President Snow recorded that during their conversation, Joseph revealed the doctrine of plurality of wives to him and said that "he foresaw the trouble that would follow, and sought to turn away from the commandment, [however] an angel from heaven then appeared before him with a drawn sword, threatening him with destruction unless he went forward and obeyed the commandment."[11] In addition to this affidavit, in a pamphlet by Joseph Fielding Smith titled, *Blood Atonement and the Origin of Plural Marriage,* it states that the LDS Church Historian's Office had more than one hun-

---

[10] *The Prophet,* 24 May 1845; cf. D&C 1981, 132:7.

[11] Smith n/d, 67–68.

dred such affidavits on file from wives and other individuals who were involved in the wedding
ceremonies—all testifying that Joseph practiced
polygamy.

It appears the most compelling reason for Joseph to live the law of polygamy, however, is the
revelation itself. Verse 3 of the revelation states:
"Therefore, prepare thy heart to receive and obey
the instructions which I am about to give unto
you; for all those who have this law revealed unto
them must obey the same."[12]

---

[12] D&C 1981, 132:3.

Chapter Four _____

Early Denials

On August 17, 1835, a general priesthood assembly of The Church of Jesus Christ of Latter-day Saints gathered in Kirtland, Ohio. The assembly was organized by Oliver Cowdery and Sidney Rigdon as members of the First Presidency of the church.[1] Joseph Smith and Frederick G. Williams, the other members of the First Presidency at that time, were absent visiting members of the church in Michigan. The sole purpose of the assembly was to approve the publication of *The Doctrine and Covenants,* and to accept it as "a law and a rule of faith and practice to the Church." The book primarily contained the revelations Joseph Smith had received from the Lord, and its publication was duly approved.[2]

The Doctrine and Covenants presented at the August 17 assembly also contained three non-revelation items, two of which are no longer in the

---

[1] The First Presidency is the ruling quorum of The Church of Jesus Christ of Latter-day Saints. All other quorums, including the Quorum of the Twelve Apostles, are subject to it.

[2] HC 1955, 2:243.

book. The two items that have been removed are "The Lectures on Faith," a compilation of lectures and instruction that had been used to educate the priesthood in Kirtland,[3] and an "Article on Marriage," which was presented at the conference by W.W. Phelps and initially accepted. The "Article on Marriage" was printed in *The Doctrine and Covenants* as Section 101 until it was deleted in 1876 and Section 132 was inserted.[4]

The third item that was not a revelation was an article entitled, "Of Governments and Laws in General," which was presented (and presumably written) by Oliver Cowdery. With some modifications, it remains in *The Doctrine and Covenants* as Section 134.

Although the "Article on Marriage" dealt with various topics, it contained a paragraph that particularly pertains to polygamy. It read as follows:

Inasmuch as this Church of Christ has been reproached with the crime of fornication and polygamy, we declare that we believe that one man should have one wife, and one woman but one husband, except in case of death, when either is at liberty to marry again.[5]

---

[3] These gatherings of the priesthood in Kirtland were known as the School of the Prophets.

[4] HC 1955, 2:243–250.

[5] HC 1955, 2:246–247 for the full Article.

This was the first formal denial of polygamy published by the LDS Church during its formative years.

It should be remembered that Joseph was not present when this article was brought before the assembly; however, he undoubtedly knew that the Article would be published in the first edition of *The Doctrine and Covenants* long before the book was sent to press since the title page of the first edition included his name, along with the names of Oliver Cowdery, Sidney Rigdon, and Frederick G. Williams as "Presiding Elders of the Church and Proprietors." In addition, the title page stated that the material in the book had been "Carefully selected from the revelations of God," and had been compiled by these men.

With the acceptance of *The Doctrine and Covenants* in 1835, the "Testimony of the Twelve Apostles to the Truth of the Book of Doctrine and Covenants" was included in the first edition and has been printed at the beginning of the book in each edition since. The names of the Twelve currently in office at that time were subscribed to this testimonial, even though they were on missions in the eastern states and were not in attendance at the assembly that approved it.[6] The book had been worked on for some time, however, and the Twelve were undoubtedly aware of the material it contained.

---

[6] The names of the Twelve Apostles were not included in the publication of the book in the *Millennial Star.* HC 1955, 2:245, ftnt.

Although the revelation on the plurality of wives was undoubtedly received as early as 1831, it is evident that Joseph did not teach the doctrine to many people during his lifetime—privately or publicly. In fact, on several occasions between 1835 and his martyrdom, he and other leaders of the church denied the existence of both the revelation on polygamy and the fact that they had taken multiple wives, as the following eight examples demonstrate:

1. August 17, 1835: The "Article on Marriage" stated, "one man should have one wife, and one woman but one husband, except in case of death, when either is at liberty to marry again."

2. May of 1836: In the *Elder's Journal,* the question was asked, "Do the Mormons believe in having more wives than one?" The answer was, "No, not at the same time."[7]

3. September 1, 1842: This statement appeared in the *Times and Seasons*: "Inasmuch as the public mind has been unjustly abused through the fallacy of Dr. [John C.] Bennett's letters, we make an extract on the subject of marriage, showing the rule of the church on this important matter. The extract is from the Book of Doctrine and Covenants, and is the only rule

---

[7] HC 1955, 5:xxx.

allowed by the Church." The article then quoted the extract verbiage from the "Article on
Marriage" noted in No. 1 above.[8]

4. March 15, 1843: The *Times and Seasons*
published an article that had appeared in the
Boston Bee. It recorded a situation where a
person who had recently joined the church
was questioned by an antagonistic nonmem-
ber. One of the statements involved an accu-
sation concerning the plurality of wives. The
Bee recorded the following response: "We are
charged with advocating a plurality of wives,
and common property. Now this is as false
as the many other ridiculous charges which
are brought against us. No sect have [sic] a
greater reverence for the laws of matrimony, or
the rights of private property, and we do what
others do not, practice what we preach."[9]

5. The following denial appeared in the LDS *Millennial Star,* Volume 3, page 74: "But, for the
information of those who may be assailed by
those foolish tales about two wives, we would
say that no such principle ever existed among
the Latter-Day Saints, and never will." It then
went on to say that "the Book of Mormon, Doctrine and Covenants; and also all our periodi-

---

[8] *Times and Seasons,* Vol. III, No. 21, p. 909.

[9] *Times and Seasons,* Vol. IV, No. 9, p. 143.

cals are very strict on that subject, indeed far more so than the [B]ible."[10]

6. On October 5, 1843, the *History of the Church* records that Joseph "[g]ave instructions to try those persons who were preaching, teaching, or practicing the doctrine of plurality of wives; for, according to the law, I hold the keys of this power in the last days; for there is never but one on earth at a time on whom the power and its keys are conferred; *and I have constantly said no man shall have but one wife at a time, unless the Lord directs otherwise.*"[11]

7. On March 15, 1844, Hyrum Smith wrote in the *Times and Seasons:* "To the brethren of the Church of Jesus Christ of [Latter-day] Saints, living on China Creek, in Hancock County, Greeting:—Whereas brother Richard Hewitt has called on me today to know my views concerning some doctrines that are preached in your place, and states to me that some of your elders say, that a man *having a certain priesthood,* may have as many wives as he pleases, and that [doctrine] is taught here: I say unto you that that man teaches *false doctrine,* for there is no such doctrine taught here; neither is there any such thing practiced here. And any man that is found teaching privately or pub-

[10] *Millennial Star,* 3:74.

[11] HC 1955, 6:46.

licly any such doctrine, is culpable, and will stand a chance to be brought before the High Council, and lose his license and membership also: therefore he had better beware what he is about."[12]

8. On May 3, 1844, Joseph was accused of keeping six or seven young females as wives. He responded: "What a thing it is for a man to be accused of committing adultery, and having seven wives, when I can only find one."[13]

Undoubtedly, other denials were published, but these are sufficient to adequately verify the fact that the church and many of its leaders were denying the existence of the revelation on celestial marriage and the practice of polygamy after it had been received and was, in fact, being practiced. However, the fact remains that the doctrine had been generally discussed prior to Brigham's public announcement in 1852, as noted from the encounter with Emma Smith quoted herein[14] and a discussion of the Nauvoo City Council concerning the *Nauvoo Expositor* wherein it was noted that one of the avowed purposes of the *Expositor* (as declared in its Prospectus) was to "decry gross moral imperfections wherever found, either

[12] *Times and Seasons*, Vol. V, No. 6, p. 474.

[13] HC 1955, 6:411.

[14] See page 18.

in the plebeian, patrician or SELF-CONSTITUT-ED MONARCH" (meaning Joseph Smith).[15] This was a clear reference to the revelation on the plurality of wives since the revelation had previously been read to the High Council of the church and had caused "much talk, about [the] multiplicity of wives."[16]

All this evidence reveals that the revelation on celestial marriage and the practice of polygamy were obviously well known by various members of the LDS Church and by many antagonists outside the church. So why did Joseph and others deny their existence (even after they had entered into polygamous relationships themselves) since their stance brought great criticism upon Joseph in particular and the church in general?

Although it is impossible to determine exactly what was in the brethren's minds at that time, there are six plausible explanations:

Ignorance: After Joseph received the revelation on the plurality of wives, he only told a few people about it. Because it was essentially kept secret for many years, it is easy to dismiss the denials in examples No. 2, 4, and 5 written previously due to a lack of knowledge on the part of those making the

[15] HC 1955, 6:443–444 for the entire Prospectus.

[16] HC 1955, 6:435.

statements. They had not heard of the revelation; consequently, their comments may have reflected the understanding they had at the time.

Restrictions: Brethren teaching doctrines that are classified as "mysteries" (doctrines that are not to be revealed until God directs) explains example No. 7. After the denial quoted in that item, Hyrum Smith continued by stating:

And again I say unto you, an elder has no business to undertake to preach mysteries in any part of the world, for God has commanded us all to preach nothing but the first principles unto the world. Neither has any elder any authority to preach any mysterious thing to any branch of the church unless he has a direct commandment from God to do so. Let the matter of the grand councils of heaven, and the making of gods, worlds, and devils *entirely alone;* **for you are not called to teach any such doctrine—for neither you nor the people are capacitated to understand any such principles—less so to teach them. For when God commands men to teach such principles the saints will receive them. Therefore beware what you teach! for the mysteries of God are not given to all men; and unto those to whom they are given**

**they are placed under restrictions to im-
part only such as God will command them;
and the residue is to be kept in a faithful
breast,** otherwise he will be brought under
condemnation. By this God will prove his
faithful servants, who will be called and
numbered *with the chosen.*[17]

Because of the reference to the doctrines of
"making of gods, worlds, and devils," it is clear
that the principles taught by the revelation were
known at this time (and maybe much earlier); however, it appears a restriction was placed on those
who knew of the doctrine which prevented them
from teaching it publicly, as explicitly noted by
Hyrum in this publication. From Hyrum's comments, three principles concerning LDS revelation
can be gleaned:

a. Revelations concerning the doctrines and prin-
    ciples of salvation may occasionally be received
    by those seeking enlightenment on those sub-
    jects for their personal use through one of two
    methods: either through direct revelation from
    the Lord through the Spirit[18] or by instruction
    from the authorities of the church pertaining
    to revelations they have received. The pub-
    lic proclamation of this information may be

---

[17] *Times and Seasons,* Vol. V, No. 6, p. 474. Bold emphasis added.

[18] See Matthew 16:17; John 14:26; *The Book of Mormon,* Alma 12:9.

restricted by God until He commands otherwise.

b. The teaching of a particular doctrine may be prohibited,[19] as is apparently the case concerning the doctrine found in Section 132 of *The Doctrine and Covenants.* This happened on other occasions during the church's early history. When the British Mission was first opened, the brethren were instructed *not* to teach the doctrine of gathering, the vision,[20] or the material published in *The Doctrine and Covenants.*[21] The Lord also prohibited certain teachings during His earthly mission. After Peter had expressed his testimony of the Savior as the Son of God, the Lord charged His disciples "that they should tell no man that he was Jesus the Christ."[22] Again, after the vision on the Mount of Transfiguration had taken place, Christ instructed Peter, James, and John to "Tell the vision to no man, until the Son of man be risen again from the dead."[23]

c. The doctrine of polygamy was known by some

[19] In revelations to Oliver Cowdery (D&C 6:9) and Hyrum Smith (D&C 11:9) in 1829 the Lord prohibited them from teaching anything but repentance at that time.

[20] Mormons interpret this to mean either the first vision of the Father and Son, or Section 76 of *The Doctrine and Covenants.*

[21] HC 1955, 2:492.

[22] Matthew 16:15–20.

[23] Matthew 17:5–9.

of the Saints and a few of the church's antagonists, but the principles involved in understanding it and the application of the commandment
itself had not been taught to the church as a
whole, nor to the world in general.

Fear: As we discussed in Chapter One, fear
of heightened persecution may have been another
reason the revelation was not publicly taught or acknowledged for many years. Joseph and the Saints
had been persecuted from the very beginning of
the restoration.[24] They had been driven from area
to area, deprived of the civil liberties guaranteed
by the Constitution, and even abused—mentally
and physically—by mobs and antagonists.[25] Considering the events of both the Kirtland and the
Missouri periods of the church's history, the public teaching and practice of a doctrine as foreign
to Christian beliefs as polygamy would have undoubtedly increased the severity of the Saints'
persecution.

Fear can cause people to do many things. Re-
member, it was fear of personal persecution and
death that caused Abraham and Isaac to hide the
identity of their wives;[26] fear resulting from the
arrest and trial of the Lord that caused Peter to

[24] Members of the LDS Church believes that Jesus Christ restored His true church
through Joseph Smith. Therefore, church members refer to the Joseph Smith period
of the church.s history and the latter days in general as "the restoration."

[25] HC 1955, 1:6–7, 263, 390; 2:103; 3:183, 411; 6:222; 7:442.

[26] Genesis 12:11–16; 26:7–10.

deny knowing the Master three times;[27] and Paul's fear of death that caused him to raise the debate between the Pharisees and the Sadducees regarding the resurrection in order to save himself from their threats.[28] Joseph and the early LDS leaders certainly had good cause to fear for their lives and for the future of the fledgling LDS Church, and that fear may have been a reason they chose to deny their early involvement in polygamy.

Complexity: As will be discussed in a later chapter, the revelation contained in Section 132 of *The Doctrine and Covenants* is a complex doctrine. It is not just about polygamy; in fact, the word "polygamy" is never mentioned in the revelation. It is about being sealed "unto eternal life." In other words, invoking the power of God to ensure the eternal salvation of mankind. It discusses the relationship between this life and mankind's continued existence throughout the eternities, and the potential for mankind to become as God is. This was a revolutionary doctrine to people living in the early 1800s, and remains so today.

Satan: Mormons believe that Satan fought the establishment of His church during the ministry of Christ and His Apostles, eventually destroying the church and bringing about what Mormons call the

---

[27] Matthew 26:70, 72, 74.

[28] Acts 23:1–9.

"great apostasy."[29] They also believe that the adversary fought the restoration of the Lord's gospel in the 1800s, including the doctrine of polygamy.

Authority: In the formative years of the church, only those who were called by Joseph Smith, as Prophet and head of the church, were authorized to practice the doctrine of polygamy. This is evident from the comment Joseph made on October 5, 1843: *"I have constantly said no man shall have but one wife at a time, unless the Lord directs otherwise."*[30] This was the position of the church throughout the period it practiced polygamy: only those directed by the Lord were officially authorized to obey the commandment found in Section 132. Once the doctrine became known, however, many abused it and participated in either acquiring multiple wives without approval or in seducing women under the pretext of the revelation (sometimes called "spiritual wifery"). This was the practice of Dr. John C. Bennett, who went about in Nauvoo teaching "that promiscuous intercourse between the sexes was a doctrine believed in by the Latter-day Saints, and that there was no harm in it."[31] Chauncey L. Higbee also taught this doctrine while he was in Nauvoo. As a result, they were both excommuni-

---

[29] Second Coming 2003, 26 et seq., for a comprehensive, referenced description of what Mormons believe caused the great apostasy and its results.

[30] HC 1955, 6:46.

[31] HC 1955, 5:36.

cated from the church.[32] Some of the members in the China Creek Branch were teaching that men holding a certain priesthood could have as many wives as they wanted. They were reprimanded by church leaders.[33] And as noted, Aaron Lyon was tried for claiming to have received a revelation directing him to marry a Sister Jackson—a married woman. He was also reprimanded.[34]

Polygamy had obviously placed Joseph and the Saints in a difficult position since the Prophet and other church leaders of the time sincerely believed that God had given them a revelation on celestial marriage. And according to their belief, when God commands you must obey. They considered the requirement of plural marriage a religious principle that was necessary for exaltation and the generation of eternal families. As a result, the church's leadership ardently and sometimes defiantly defended this principle against all who would attack it, as will be seen in the next chapter.

---

[32] HC 1955, 5:18, 75–81.

[33] *Time & Seasons*, Vol. V, No. 6, p. 474.

[34] HC 1955, 3:28.

Chapter Five _____
God's Hand In All Things

Men and women began to persecute Joseph Smith as soon as they heard about his vision of the Father and the Son. His response to that persecution is recorded in his history:

> Why persecute me for telling the truth? I have actually seen a vision; and who am I that I can withstand God, or why does the world think to make me deny what I have actually seen? For I had seen a vision; I knew it, and I knew that God knew it, and I could not deny it, neither dared I do it; at least I knew that by so doing I would offend God, and come under condemnation.[1]

And as soon as people heard about the practice of polygamy, the persecution increased.

Many factors led to the Prophet's final arrest and martyrdom, but polygamy (or 'spiritual

_____
[1] *The Pearl of Great Price*, Joseph Smith—History 1:25.

wifery' as it was called by the Prophet's antagonists) and the destruction of the *Nauvoo Expositor* were the main causes. Nonetheless, his death
did not destroy the church or its doctrines, and
polygamy continued—albeit in secret—until the
practice was publicly acknowledged by Brigham
Young in 1852.

Brigham Young and his successors faced the
same problems Joseph had encountered. They knew
the practice of polygamy would cause problems for
both the Saints who practiced it and the church
that advocated it. But they also believed it was a
commandment from God, and that those who had
the law revealed to them must obey it. As verse
4 of the revelation succinctly states, "... I reveal
unto you a new and an everlasting covenant; and
if ye abide not that covenant, then are ye damned;
for no one can reject this covenant and be permitted to enter into my glory."[2] Despite their eventual ambiguity, the following quotes show that these
edicts were deeply imbedded in the souls of the
early Saints.

Brigham Young

"We are told that if we would give up polygamy—which we know to be a doctrine revealed
from heaven . . . but suppose this Church should
give up this holy order of marriage, then would the
devil, and all who are in league with him against

[2] D&C 1981, 132:4.

the cause of God, rejoice that they had prevailed upon the Saints to refuse to obey one of the revelations and commandments of God. . . . Will the Latter-day Saints do this? No; they will not to please anybody."[3]

"Now if any of you will deny the plurality of wives and continue to do so, I promise that you will be damned . . ."[4]

Lorenzo Snow

When President Snow was on trial for the practice of polygamy, Mr. Bierbower, the prosecuting attorney, predicted that if he were convicted, "a new revelation would soon follow, changing the divine law of celestial marriage." To this President Snow responded: "Whatever fame Mr. Bierbower may have secured as a lawyer, he certainly will fail as a prophet. . . . Though I go to prison God will not change his law of celestial marriage. But the man, the people, the nation, that oppose and fight against this doctrine and the Church of God, will be overthrown."[5]

John Taylor

"God has given us a revelation in regard to celestial marriage. I did not make it. . . they would like us to tone that principle down and change

---

[3] JD 1967, 11:239.

[4] *Deseret Evening News,* 14 November 1855.

[5] LDS Church Historical Department, *Historical Record,* 1886, Vol 5:144.

it and make it applicable to the views of the day. This we cannot do; nor can we interfere with any of the commands of God to meet the persuasions or behests of men. I cannot do it, and will not do it. I find some men try to twist round the principle in any way and every way they can. They want to sneak out of it in some way. Now God don't [sic] want any kind of sycophancy like that."[6]

Heber C. Kimball
"You might as well deny 'Mormonism,' and turn away from it, as to oppose the plurality of wives. Let the Presidency of this Church, and the Twelve Apostles, and all the authorities unite and say with one voice that they will oppose that doctrine, and the whole of them would be damned."[7]

Wilford Woodruff
"If we were to do away with polygamy, it would only be one feather in the bird, one ordinance in the Church and kingdom. Do away with that, then we must do away with prophets and Apostles, with revelation and the gifts and graces of the Gospel, and finally give up our religion altogether and turn sectarians and do as the world does then all would be right. We just can't do that. . . . We shall obey Him in days to come as we have in days past."[8]

[6] JD 1967, 25:309.

[7] JD 1967, 5:203.

[8] JD 1967, 13:166.

Joseph F. Smith

"I understand the law of celestial marriage to mean that every man in this Church, who has the ability to obey and practice it in righteousness and will not, shall be damned, I say I understand it to mean this and nothing less, and I testify in the name of Jesus that it does mean that."[9]

Why did these men make these statements? Because they believed God had commanded them to live the law of celestial marriage, and they believed that if they stopped without His directive— as their persecutors demanded—they would be rejecting God.

There is an interesting example in the Old Testament that can perhaps shed light on the reasoning of the brethren as they recorded their beliefs. Moses was called by God to deliver Israel from bondage. To that end, God commanded him to go to Pharaoh and demand that Pharaoh let the children of Israel go. Moses did as he was commanded, but Pharaoh's answer to Moses' demands was declaratory: "Who is the Lord, that I should obey his voice to let Israel go? I know not the Lord, neither will I let Israel go."[10] What was Moses to do? Walk away? He could not. He had been commanded by God to deliver the Israelites

---

[9] JD 1967, 20:31.

[10] Exodus 5:2.

from bondage, so he kept on following the Lord's directives until Pharaoh finally let the children of Israel go.

In the New Testament, Paul taught that anyone (himself included) who preached "any other gospel" than that which the Savior taught would be "accursed." As he boldly declared to the Romans: ". . . I am not ashamed of the gospel of Christ: for it is the power of God unto salvation to every one that believeth." [11]

In like manner, Joseph Smith and his followers could not just walk away from the commandments found in the 132nd Section of *The Doctrine and Covenants.* So they preached and lived the doctrine as best they could, in spite of open persecution. They believed that the eternal covenant of marriage—which included polygamy—was part of the restoration of all things.

In spite of the severe persecution they had suffered, the Mormons believed that God had delivered them from their enemies in and around Palmyra, New York; Kirtland, Ohio; Jackson County, Missouri; and Nauvoo, Illinois. Their belief motivated them to follow their prophet from state to state in an attempt to preserve their identity and live the Lord's commandments. After Joseph's death, they were again forced to leave all they had built and under the direction of Brigham Young, the major-

---

[11] Galatians 1:8; Romans 1:16.

ity of them moved to the Great Salt Lake Valley, a place where they could grow and flourish. And grow and flourish they did (ironically with the aid of polygamy) until they were so strong they could not be driven out.

The Saints built a thriving city in the Great Salt Lake Valley almost overnight. One hundred forty-eight men, women, and children entered the valley on July 24, 1847. By 1870 the population had risen to 12,000, and by 1890 it was up to 45,000.[12] In addition, thousands of other members spread out rapidly, establishing communities in other undeveloped areas of the West. Enduring enormous hardships, they also built churches and temples where they could worship according to their beliefs.

When the Saints' enemies recognized that they could not physically displace the church, they attempted to destroy it and its practices through legislation. However, the church believed—and still believes—that the Constitution of the United States was divinely inspired, and they relied upon it for protection. Now firmly ensconced in the Great Basin after having been driven out of four states, they were determined not to relinquish the Territory of Utah. So they fought, not physically with swords and guns, but legally—defending

---

[12] John S. McCormick, *Salt Lake City, The Gathering Place: An Illustrated History* (Salt Lake City: Signature Books, 1980); "Salt Lake City," *Utah History Encyclopedia* (Salt Lake City: University of Utah Press, 1994).

their religious and civil freedoms under the law. In the end, however, members of the LDS Church believe that the Lord finally accepted the Saints' offerings of obedience (as he had when they had attempted to establish Zion[13]) and revealed that the practice of polygamy would cease. This may seem like a dichotomy in view of the above quotes from LDS Church leaders, but there are multiple scriptures that indicate the Lord does occasionally change His mind.[14]

Was it the government's relentless persecution of the LDS Church that caused the Lord to end the practice of polygamy? Yes. Did the revelation that ended the practice of plural marriage also end the belief in the doctrine of celestial marriage? No. The Mormon belief in Section 132 has survived, but the *practice* of polygamy, has not.

---

[13] D&C 124:49–51

[14] Numbers 14:23–34; 2 Kings 20:1–11, 22:14 et seq.; Isaiah 38:1–8; D&C 56:4.

Chapter Six _____
The Revelation

Because Section 132 of *The Doctrine and Covenants* is the source of authority used by Joseph Smith and his successors for the practice of polygamy, we will examine it in detail in this chapter. Before doing so, however, it is important to consider the following two positions.

First: The members of the Church of Jesus Christ of Latter-day Saints believe that Joseph Smith was a prophet, that he received the revelation on celestial marriage from God, and that he continued to receive revelations during the restoration of the gospel. (They also believe that LDS prophets receive revelation today.) Because of this belief, Mormons sustain Section 132 as part of the official doctrine of their church.[1]

Second: From its inception, there have always been antagonists against the practice of polygamy and many have questioned, and continue to question, whether Joseph received the revelation con-

---

[1] For a detailed review of the authorship of Section 132 in *The Doctrine and Covenants*, see HC 1955, 5:xxix–xlvi.

tained in Section 132. It is important to note that most other Christian religions in Joseph's time (and many today) believed prophetic revelation ended with the Bible. As a result, it is little wonder that when he claimed to receive open visions from God, many disbelieved him, and when he started to attract followers, people actually started to fear and hate him. However, prior to his death his enemies accused him more of adultery, espousing polygamist doctrine, and instigating the practice of plural wives than of receiving the revelation that started it all. Break offs from the church after his death either claimed he was a fallen prophet or that Section 132 and the practice of polygamy originated with Brigham Young.[2]

It is not the purview of this work to prove or disprove the authenticity of Joseph's revelations, but to provide insight into an historical doctrine of the LDS Church that has had—and apparently will continue to have—a significant religious and political impact. To that end, we will now go through the revelation in detail.[3]

---

[2] The largest break off from the LDS Church, The Reorganized Church of Jesus Christ of Latter Day Saints, was organized after Joseph Smith's death. Its members questioned whether Joseph received Section 132 of *The Doctrine and Covenants* from the Lord.

[3] It should be clearly understood that as the author, I am solely responsible for the interpretation of the following verses. Although my comments are based on extensive research, I do not speak for the LDS Church.

Section 132
The Doctrine and Covenants
(Author comments in italics following verses)

¹Verily, thus saith the Lord unto you my servant Joseph, that inasmuch as you have inquired of my hand to know and understand wherein I, the Lord, justified my servants Abraham, Isaac, and Jacob, as also Moses, David and Solomon, my servants, as touching the principle and doctrine of their having many wives and concubines—²Behold, and lo, I am the Lord thy God, and will answer thee as touching this matter. ³Therefore, prepare thy heart to receive and **obey** the instructions which I am about to give unto you; **for all those who have this law revealed unto them must obey the same** [emphasis added].

(1–3) After reading about the Old Testament practice of polygamy, Joseph's curious nature motivated him to ask the Lord why those practices were not considered adulterous. Having previously read in James 1:5 that anyone lacking wisdom could "ask of God, that giveth to all men liberally, and upbraideth not," he proceeded with his inquiry. He had successfully used this procedure many times up to this point.

⁴For behold, I reveal unto you a new and an everlasting covenant; and if ye abide not that covenant, then are ye damned; for no one can reject this covenant and be permitted to enter into my glory. ⁵For all who will have a blessing at my hands shall abide the law which was appointed for that blessing, and the conditions thereof, as were instituted from before the foundation of the world. ⁶And as pertaining to the new and everlasting covenant, it was instituted for the fulness of my glory; and he that receiveth a fulness thereof must and shall abide the law, or he shall be damned, saith the Lord God.

(4–6) The LDS Church teaches that to be held accountable for a commandment, you must first receive it and understand it and then be aware of the blessings you will receive if you keep it—and the consequences if you disobey it. Verses 3–4 make it clear that those who receive this revelation must comply with its parameters. Those who choose to disobey will be "damned" (from the Mormon perspective, this means not to be allowed back into the presence of the Father and be exalted in His kingdom.) (See also D&C 1981, 130:20–21.)

7And verily I say unto you, that the conditions of this law are these: All covenants, contracts, bonds, obligations, oaths, vows, performances, connections, associations, or expectations, that are not made and entered into and sealed by the Holy Spirit of promise, of him who is anointed, both as well for time and for all eternity, and that too most holy, by revelation and commandment through the medium of mine anointed, whom I have appointed on the earth to hold this power (and I have appointed unto my servant Joseph to hold this power in the last days, and there is never but one on the earth at a time on whom this power and the keys of this priesthood are conferred), are of no efficacy, virtue, or force in and after the resurrection from the dead; for all contracts that are not made unto this end have an end when men are dead.

(7) Mormons believe that marriage and the family unit can last beyond this earthly life, but to receive this blessing, the marriage must be performed by an authorized member of the LDS priesthood and sealed (approved of or accepted) by the Holy Spirit. Latter-day Saints believe the Lord gave this authority to Joseph Smith and that it is given to only one man at a time on the earth, the prophet and president of the LDS Church, who presides over all offices, doctrines and procedures of the church and may delegate this au-

thority to men who serve in LDS temples for the purpose of performing marriages, and to other men as required. (See D&C 28:7; 107:66–67.) Without priesthood authority and the seal of the Holy Spirit, a marriage is considered valid only while husband and wife live on this earth.

⁸Behold, mine house is a house of order, saith the Lord God, and not a house of confusion. ⁹Will I accept an offering, saith the Lord, that is not made in my name? ¹⁰Or will I receive at your hands that which I have not appointed? ¹¹And will I appoint unto you, saith the Lord, except it be by law, even as I and my Father ordained unto you, before the world was?

(8–11) These verses anticipate the Lord's answers in subsequent verses. It implies that the Lord will accept nothing except that which is done in His name. (See 1 Kings 18: 19–38 where the Lord refuses to accept the sacrifices of the false prophets of Baal, but does accept the offering done in His name by the prophet Elijah. The LDS Church believes that Joseph Smith was foreordained in the pre-existence to be a prophet, as was Jeremiah.) (Jeremiah 1:5.)

¹²I am the Lord thy God; and I give unto you this commandment—that no man shall come unto the Father but by me or by my word, which is my law, saith the Lord. ¹³And everything that is in the world, whether it be ordained of men, by thrones, or principalities, or powers, or things of name, whatsoever they may be, that are not by me or by my word, saith the Lord, shall be thrown down, and shall not remain after men are dead, neither in nor after the resurrection, saith the Lord your God. ¹⁴For whatsoever things remain are by me; and whatsoever things are not by me shall be shaken and destroyed.

(12–14) The Lord assuredly knew that this revela-

tion would be controversial, so it is understandable that He would emphasize the sobriety of His message by re-affirming that only through obedience to His laws could a man or woman return to the presence of our Heavenly Father. Mormons believe that without the Lord's author-ity, no blessing obtained on this earth will be recognized after the resurrection.

15Therefore, if a man mar-ry him a wife in the world, and he marry her not by me nor by my word, and he cov-enant with her so long as he is in the world and she with him, their covenant and mar-riage are not of force when they are dead, and when they are out of the world; there-fore, they are not bound by any law when they are out of the world. **16**Therefore, when they are out of the world they neither marry nor are giv-en in marriage; but are ap-pointed angels in heaven, which angels are minister-ing servants, to minister for those who are worthy of a far more, and an exceeding, and an eternal weight of glo-ry. **17**For these angels did not abide my law; therefore, they cannot be enlarged, but remain separately and singly, without exaltation, in their saved condition, to all eter-nity; and from henceforth are not gods, but are angels of God forever and ever.

(15–17) Mormons believe that men and women who fail to have their marriages performed by the proper author-ity and sealed by the Holy Spirit will not remain married after the resurrection. They are, nevertheless, "saved," al-though they will serve as ministering angels to those whose marriages were sealed by the Holy Spirit. Most Christian churches appeal to the Gospel of Matthew, Chapter 22, verses 24–30, to support their belief that there will be no marriages or paired unions in heaven. Members of the LDS Church believe the Lord clarified those verses here.

18And again, verily I say   unto you, if a man marry a

wife, and make a covenant with her for time and for all eternity, if that covenant is not by me or by my word, which is my law, and is not sealed by the Holy Spirit of promise, through him whom I have anointed and appointed unto this power, then it is not valid neither of force when they are out of the world, because they are not joined by me, saith the Lord, neither by my word; when they are out of the world it cannot be received there, because the angels and the gods are appointed there, by whom they cannot pass; they cannot, therefore, inherit my glory; for my house is a house of order, saith the Lord God.

(18) One of the most ardent claims by members of the LDS Church is that the true church of Jesus Christ is defined by authorized priesthood authority and obedience to the laws of God. Verse 18 is therefore an important component of the revelation authorizing polygamous marriages because it underscores the need for authorization by the one man on earth who has the power to grant it—the Lord's prophet (see verse 7). Without this authority the marriage is not valid.

¹⁹And again, verily I say unto you, if a man marry a wife by my word, which is my law, and by the new and everlasting covenant, and it is sealed unto them by the Holy Spirit of promise, by him who is anointed, unto whom I have appointed this power and the keys of this priesthood; and it shall be said unto them—Ye shall come forth in the first resurrection; and if it be after the first resurrection, in the next resurrection; and shall inherit thrones, kingdoms, principalities, and powers, dominions, all heights and depths—then shall it be written in the Lamb's Book of Life, that he shall commit no murder whereby to shed innocent blood, and if ye abide in my covenant, and commit no murder whereby to shed innocent blood, it shall be done unto them in all things whatsoever my servant hath put upon them, in time, and through

all eternity; and shall be of full force when they are out of the world; and they shall pass by the angels, and the gods, which are set there, to their exaltation and glory in all things, as hath been sealed upon their heads, which glory shall be a fulness and a continuation of the seeds forever and ever. [20]Then shall they be gods, because they have no end; therefore shall they be from everlasting to everlasting, because they continue; then shall they be above all, because all things are subject unto them. Then shall they be gods, because they have all power, and the angels are subject unto them. [21]Verily, verily, I say unto you, except ye abide my law ye cannot attain to this glory.

(19–21) These are perhaps three of the most controversial verses in Mormon scripture. The LDS Church teaches that all men and women are God's spiritual children and as such, have the capacity and opportunity to become like Him—to become gods themselves. This is a doctrine expressed by the psalmist (Psalms 82:6), used by the Lord when confronted by the Jewish rulers during his good shepherd discourse (John 10:34–36), and at least referred to by Paul in his Epistle to the Corinthians. (See 1 Cor. 8:5.) Mormons believe husbands and wives who have been married by proper authority and had their marriages sealed by the Holy Spirit, and who obey the Lord's laws and do not commit murder, will come forth in the first or "next" resurrection (the resurrection of the just) into the kingdom of God.[†] They believe they will be exalted in the Father's kingdom (See Romans 8:16–17; Galatians 4:7) and be privileged to produce spirit children (a "continuation of the seeds forever and ever"). Mormons believe this means they will be able to procreate in the eternities.

[†] See D&C 1981, 76:51–70, 92–95. Matthew 20:1–16; JC 1959: 482, 508; Cunningham Geikie, *The Life and Words of Christ,* revised ed., 2 vols. (New York: Appleton & Company, 1891, 1894), 2:357; Ed 1981: 2:416–418; Trench n.d.: 63, 65; Frederic W. Farrar, *The Life of Christ,* 2 vols. (New York: E.P. Dutton & Company, 1874) 2:164.

22For strait is the gate, and narrow the way that leadeth unto the exaltation and continuation of the lives, and few there be that find it, because ye receive me not in the world neither do ye know me. **23**But if ye receive me in the world, then shall ye know me, and shall receive your exaltation; that where I am ye shall be also. **24**This is eternal lives—to know the only wise and true God, and Jesus Christ, whom he hath sent. I am he. Receive ye, therefore, my law. **25**Broad is the gate, and wide the way that leadeth to the deaths; and many there are that go in thereat, because they receive me not, neither do they abide in my law.

(22–25) Jesus declares that it is He who is speaking in this revelation and He commands Joseph and all the Saints to "receive" (live) His law. According to LDS Doctrine, you only come to know Jesus Christ and His Father by living Their commandments. If you accept Christ, you must obey His laws. The narrow and broad gate and/or way comparison is again used to illustrate the number who are willing to obey God's law as compared to the number who will reject it. (See Matthew 7:14; John 14:1–3, 17:3.)

26Verily, verily, I say unto you, if a man marry a wife according to my word, and they are sealed by the Holy Spirit of promise, according to mine appointment, and he or she shall commit any sin or transgression of the new and everlasting covenant whatever, and all manner of blasphemies, and if they commit no murder wherein they shed innocent blood, yet they shall come forth in the first resurrection, and enter into their exaltation; but they shall be destroyed in the flesh, and shall be delivered unto the buffetings of Satan unto the day of redemption, saith the Lord God. **27**The blasphemy against the Holy Ghost, which shall not be forgiven in the world nor out of the world, is in that ye commit murder wherein ye shed innocent blood, and assent unto my death, after ye have received my new and everlasting covenant, saith the Lord God; and he that abideth not this law can in nowise enter into my glory, but shall be damned, saith the Lord. [28]I am the Lord thy God, and will give unto thee the law of my Holy Priesthood, as was ordained by me and my Father before the world was.

(26–28) Mormons believe being married for time and eternity by the proper authority and being sealed by the Holy Spirit of promise are requirements for exaltation. For those who are worthy of exaltation, their "calling and election" are made sure (2 Peter 1:10), meaning the Lord has judged them while they are on this earth and their exaltation has been approved. Should they sin after this point, they will suffer punishment in this life rather than having their sins absolved by the Atonement of Christ. That suffering, described in the revelation as being "destroyed in the flesh" and "delivered unto the buffetings of Satan," has never been defined by the Lord. However, members of the LDS Church believe this guarantee of exaltation will only be revoked if elected men or women commit murder, the "shedding of innocent blood," which the Lord defines as an unforgivable blasphemy against the Holy Ghost and a denial of the only Begotten Son of the Father, wherein they crucify Him unto themselves and put Him to an open shame. (See D&C 1981, 76:35.) Mormons believe that people guilty of such a transgression qualify for damnation (or "outer darkness") where they will receive no glory and will become "sons of perdition" (D&C 1981, 76:25–49; John 17:12) for eternity.

The Lord is now going to lay the foundation for His law of polygamy.

[29]Abraham received all things, whatsoever he received, by revelation and commandment, by my word, saith the Lord, and hath entered into his ex-

altation and sitteth upon his throne. [30]Abraham received promises concerning his seed, and of the fruit of his loins—from whose loins ye are, namely, my servant Joseph—which were to continue so long as they were in the world; and as touching Abraham and his seed, out of the world they should continue; both in the world and out of the world should they continue as innumerable as the stars; or, if ye were to count the sand upon the seashore ye could not number them. [31]This promise is yours also, because ye are of Abraham, and the promise was made unto Abraham; and by this law is the continuation of the works of my Father, wherein he glorifieth himself. [32]Go ye, therefore, and do the works of Abraham; enter ye into my law and ye shall be saved. [33]But if ye enter not into my law ye cannot receive the promise of my Father, which he made unto Abraham. [34]God commanded Abraham, and Sarah gave Hagar to Abraham to wife. And why did she do it? Because this was the law; and from Hagar sprang many people. This, therefore, was fulfilling, among other things, the promises. [35]Was Abraham, therefore, under condemnation? Verily I say unto you, Nay; for I, the Lord, commanded it.

(29–35) Mormons believe Abraham complied with God's law and has achieved exaltation. He was promised innumerable descendants and that promise has been kept. Since Joseph Smith is one of Abraham's descendants, the promises inherent in the Covenant of Abraham extend to him, and through him and the keys of the priesthood which he held, to all the Saints.

Note that God commanded Abraham to receive Hagar. Sarah complied with this because she knew the law was from God. As a result, a portion of the Covenant of Abraham (being blessed with numerous seed, or descendants) was fulfilled. All religions believe that the children of God are justified in their obedience to His commandments. Jo-

seph Smith believed—and church members today believe— that the Lord gave this revelation and therefore, Joseph and the members were required to live it. Prior to verse 34, the Lord discussed and defined the concept of eternal marriage, but beginning with verse 34, He expanded His commandments to justify plural wives. The remainder of Section 132 contains the verses the LDS Church uses to justify its belief in polygamy.

36Abraham was commanded to offer his son Isaac; nevertheless, it was written: Thou shalt not kill. Abraham, however, did not refuse, and it was accounted unto him for righteousness. **37**Abraham received concubines, and they bore him children; and it was accounted unto him for righteousness, because they were given unto him, and he abode in my law; as Isaac also and Jacob did none other things than that which they were commanded; and because they did none other things than that which they were commanded, they have entered into their exaltation, according to the promises, and sit upon thrones, and are not angels but are gods. **38**David also received many wives and concubines, and also Solomon and Moses my servants, as also many others of my servants, from the beginning of creation until this time; and in nothing did they sin save in those things which they received not of me. **39**David's wives and concubines were given unto him of me, by the hand of Nathan, my servant, and others of the prophets who had the keys of this power; and in none of these things did he sin against me save in the case of Uriah and his wife; and, therefore he hath fallen from his exaltation, and received his portion; and he shall not inherit them out of the world, for I gave them unto another, saith the Lord.

(36–39) In these verses, the Lord begins answering Joseph's initial question: How were the ancients justified in having multiple wives? Verse 36 leads by providing an

example of Abraham's righteousness when he followed the command of God to sacrifice his son Isaac. Verse 37 continues by justifying Abraham and others having plural wives because they were obedient to God and were doing only that which they were commanded to do. Verse 38 introduces an important example for the law of plural wives: David had many wives and concubines given to him by Nathan and other prophets (Samuel 12:8–11), but in the case of Bathsheba and her husband Uriah, he sinned. Bathsheba was not given to him by the prophet and David had Uriah killed through treachery during a military campaign. Therefore, he lost his wives and concubines and they were given to another.

[40]I am the Lord thy God, and I gave unto thee, my servant Joseph, an appointment, and restore all things. Ask what ye will, and it shall be given unto you according to my word. [41]And as ye have asked concerning adultery, verily, verily, I say unto you, if a man receiveth a wife in the new and everlasting covenant, and if she be with another man, and I have not appointed unto her by the holy anointing, she hath committed adultery and shall be destroyed. [42]If she be not in the new and everlasting covenant, and she be with another man, she has committed adultery. [43]And if her husband be with another woman, and he was under a vow, he hath broken his vow and hath committed adultery. [44]And if she hath not committed adultery, but is innocent and hath not broken her vow, and she knoweth it, and I reveal it unto you, my servant Joseph, then shall you have power, by the power of my Holy Priesthood, to take her and give her unto him that hath not committed adultery but hath been faithful; for he shall be made ruler over many.

(40–44) These verses are important as they define (with verses 61–65) the limits of polygamous marriages. Most religions agree that any intimate association between

a husband and another woman, or a wife and another man, is adultery. However, men and women are free to marry once all previous associations are dissolved via divorce or the death of a spouse. Polygamy necessarily complicates these requirements, and the Lord resolves these complications in these verses. Verse 41 teaches that once a husband and wife have been sealed together under the new and everlasting covenant of marriage, the woman cannot then be with another man without the blessing of the Lord. This implies that she could be with another man with the Lord's blessing. This gives rise to three possibilities: (A) The wife is permitted to remarry after the death of her husband (today, the LDS Church interprets this verse to mean a woman can be married for "time only" after the death of her husband, to whom she has been sealed). (B) If a divorce has occurred, a wife can be sealed anew if the prior sealing has been cancelled. (C) A condition known as polyandry (the marriage of multiple men to one wife) may be permitted. Verse 42 states clearly that if a husband and wife are married but not sealed together under the new and everlasting covenant of marriage, the woman cannot be with another man under any circumstances so long as the marriage exists (and presumably both partners are alive). Verse 43 teaches that if a husband is with another woman and "under a vow" (this could mean a worldly or civil marriage as well as being sealed), he is committing adultery (again presuming both parties are alive and the marriage intact). Because these conditions and circumstances are complex, the Lord provided a process in verse 44 to further resolve questions of fidelity.

⁴⁵For I have conferred upon you the keys and power of the priesthood, wherein I restore all things, and make known unto you all things in due time. ⁴⁶And verily, verily, I say unto you, that whatsoever you seal on earth shall be sealed in heaven; and whatsoever you bind on earth, in my

name and by my word, saith the Lord, it shall be eternally bound in the heavens; and whosesoever sins you remit on earth shall be remitted eternally in the heavens; and whosesoever sins you retain on earth shall be retained in heaven. [47]And again, verily I say, whomsoever you bless I will bless, and whomsoever you curse I will curse, saith the Lord; for I, the Lord, am thy God.

(45–47) The Lord acknowledges that Joseph has received the keys of the priesthood, but indicates there are things yet to be restored. He is granted what LDS Church members call the "sealing authority"—the ability to seal or bind both on earth and in heaven. (See Matthew 16:19 where the Lord gave the same power [expanded here] to Peter.) There is a condition, however. The binding must be in the Lord's name and by His "word," implying that it must comply with all of the requirements of the Lord's law pertaining to this subject (i.e., being sealed by the Holy Spirit of Promise).

[48]And again, verily I say unto you, my servant Joseph, that whatsoever you give on earth, and to whomsoever you give any one on earth, by my word and according to my law, it shall be visited with blessings and not cursings, and with my power, saith the Lord, and shall be without condemnation on earth and in heaven.

(48) The Lord grants Joseph the power to give additional wives to qualified men as He (the Lord) directs, so long as it is in accordance with His law.

[49]For I am the Lord they God, and will be with thee even unto the end of the world, and through all eternity; for verily I seal upon you your exaltation, and prepare a throne for you in the kingdom of my Father, with Abraham your father.

(49) Mormons interpret this verse to mean that Joseph's calling and election were made sure by the Lord. (See verses 26–28.)

⁵⁰Behold, I have seen your sacrifices, and will forgive all your sins; I have seen your sacrifices in obedience to that which I have told you. Go, therefore, and I make a way for your escape, as I accepted the offering of Abraham of his son Isaac.

(50) By 1842 when the information in this verse was recorded, Joseph had already taken multiple wives. The Lord affirms this in his blessing to Joseph wherein He states, "I have seen your sacrifices in obedience to that which I have told you." Joseph and the other church leaders undoubtedly knew the difficulties polygamy would cause and the Lord comforted Joseph by telling him that He would provide a way for him to overcome the problems created by accepting and living His law.

⁵¹Verily, I say unto you: A commandment I give unto mine handmaid, Emma Smith, your wife, whom I have given unto you, that she stay herself and partake not of that which I commanded you to offer unto her; for I did it, saith the Lord, to prove you all, as I did Abraham, and that I might require an offering at your hand, by covenant and sacrifice.

(51) There is no information available to indicate what Joseph had been commanded to offer Emma. Whatever it was, the Lord revoked the requirement.

⁵²And let mine handmaid, Emma Smith, receive all those that have been given unto my servant Joseph, and who are virtuous and pure before me; and those who are not pure, and have said they were pure, shall be de-

stroyed, saith the Lord God. [53]For I am the Lord thy God, and ye shall obey my voice; and I give unto my servant Joseph that he shall be made ruler over many things; for he hath been faithful over a few things, and from henceforth I will strengthen him. [54]And I command mine handmaid, Emma Smith, to abide and cleave unto my servant Joseph, and to none else. But if she will not abide this commandment she shall be destroyed, saith the Lord; for I am the Lord thy God, and will destroy her if she abide not in my law. [55]But if she will not abide this commandment, then shall my servant Joseph do all things for her, even as he hath said; and I will bless him and multiply him and give unto him an hundredfold in this world, of fathers and mothers, brothers and sisters, houses and lands, wives and children, and crowns of eternal lives in the eternal worlds. [56]And again, verily I say, let mine handmaid forgive my servant Joseph his trespasses; and then shall she be forgiven her trespasses, wherein she has trespassed against me; and I, the Lord thy God, will bless her, and multiply her, and make her heart to rejoice.

(52–56) These verses contain the Lord's commandment to Emma that she participate in plural marriage. It is obvious from verse 52 that the prophet had multiple wives by this time. As noted, Emma was reluctant to accept the law. Consequently, she was given a general warning that she must obey Joseph and the law or she, too, would be destroyed.[†]

[57]And again, I say, let not my servant Joseph put his prop- erty out of his hands, lest an enemy come and destroy him;

[†] See the parable of the unmerciful servant: Matthew 18:23–35; Ed 1981: 1:561, 563–564, 2:293, 296; JC 1959: 261–262, 394–395; Alexander Balmain Bruce, *A Systematic and Critical Study of the Parables of Our Lord*, 7th ed. (London: Hodder and Stoughton, 1897), 238–9, 401; Trench n.d., 55, 104; Spencer W. Kimball, *Faith Precedes the Miracle* (Salt Lake City: Deseret Book, 1972), 193–194; Spencer W. Kimball, *The Miracle of Forgiveness* (Salt Lake City: Bookcraft, 1969), 59, 269.

for Satan seeketh to destroy; for I am the Lord thy God, and he is my servant; and behold, and lo, I am with him, as I was with Abraham, thy father, even unto his exaltation and glory.

(57) Compare to Luke 22:31.

[58]Now, as touching the law of the priesthood, there are many things pertaining thereunto. [59]Verily, if a man be called of my Father, as was Aaron, by mine own voice, and by the voice of him that sent me, and I have endowed him with the keys of the power of this priesthood, if he do anything in my name, and according to my law and by my word, he will not commit sin, and I will justify him. [60]Let no one, therefore, set on my servant Joseph; for I will justify him; for he shall do the sacrifice which I require at his hands for his transgressions, saith the Lord your God.

(58–60) These verses clarify that it is not sinful to abide the law of the new and everlasting covenant of marriage if it is done according to the Savior's word and the law He has instituted. The Lord notes that no one should "set on," or in other words, condemn Joseph because he complied with the Lord's commandments, particularly the commandment to live the law of polygamy. The Lord has justified Joseph and He alone has the right to punish Joseph for any transgressions he may have committed.

[61]And again, as pertaining to the law of the priesthood—if any man espouse a virgin, and desire to espouse another, and the first give her consent, and if he espouse the second, and they are virgins, and have vowed to no other man, then is he justified; he cannot commit adultery for they are given unto him; for he cannot commit adultery with that that belongeth unto him and to no one else. [62]And if he have ten virgins given unto him by this law, he

cannot commit adultery, for they belong to him, and they are given unto him; therefore is he justified. [63]But if one or either of the ten virgins, after she is espoused, shall be with another man, she has committed adultery, and shall be destroyed; for they are given unto him to multiply and replenish the earth, according to my commandment, and to fulfil the promise which was given by my Father before the foundation of the world, and for their exaltation in the eternal worlds, that they may bear the souls of men; for herein is the work of my Father continued, that he may be glorified. [64]And again, verily, verily, I say unto you, if any man have a wife, who holds the keys of this power, and he teaches unto her the law of my priesthood, as pertaining to these things, then shall she believe and administer unto him, or she shall be destroyed, saith the Lord your God; for I will destroy her; for I will magnify my name upon all those who receive and abide in my law. [65]Therefore, it shall be lawful in me, if she receive not this law, for him to receive all things whatsoever I, the Lord his God, will give unto him, because she did not believe and administer unto him according to my word; and she then becomes the transgressor; and he is exempt from the law of Sarah, who administered unto Abraham according to the law when I commanded Abraham to take Hagar to wife. [66]And now, as pertaining to this law, verily, verily, I say unto you, I will reveal more unto you, hereafter; therefore, let this suffice for the present. Behold, I am Alpha and Omega. Amen.

The Law of Sarah

(61–66) The law of plural marriage requires no more and no less from mankind than any of God's other laws. For instance, Adam and Eve were initially told they could eat of all the fruit in the Garden of Eden.[4] Then the Lord told them they could not eat from the fruit of the tree of knowledge of good and evil,[5] cautioning them that if they did, they would die. Adam and Eve could either obey and live in God's presence, or disobey and accept the punishment.

This was the requirement that was placed upon the men and women who were called to live the law of plural marriage in the early days of the LDS Church[6]—they could either obey and gain the reward, or disobey and accept the punishment, a concept that early church leaders knew well and believed.[7]

While members of the church before the Manifesto of 1890 were required to abide by the law of plural marriage, the law did not justify arbitrary marriages. Men could not seek polygamous marriages without first having been properly selected to do so. Moreover, if they asked to be selected, they could be denied.[8]

---

[4] Genesis 2:16.

[5] Genesis 2:17.

[6] See verses 3–6.

[7] See Chapter 5, pages 42–45.

[8] D&C 132:19 and HC 1955, 3:28.

The law of plural marriage also required the husband to show respect to his first wife by consulting her concerning a new marriage and seek her consent. The rules governing this consultation are found in verses 61–66 and are collectively called the *law of Sarah,* one of the most controversial requirements of the law of eternal marriage as taught in Section 132. The law honors Abraham's wife Sarah, who agreed to abide in a polygamous relationship with Hagar, her servant, so that Abraham could have children.

The consultation a husband must hold with his first wife[9] is reflected in the church's modern teachings concerning family councils.[10] The law of Sarah requires the husband to teach his wife the law revealed in Section 132 — i.e., that he has been commanded to live the law of plural marriage and is willing to obey that commandment. Second, the wife is commanded to believe the law, which means she must accept the commandment along with her husband if they are to reap the Lord's reward. Third, the wife must "administer" to her husband, meaning she agrees to support her husband in his desire to obey the Lord just as Sarah "administered unto Abraham according to the law when [the Lord] commanded Abraham to take Hagar to wife."[11]

---

[9] See verse 61.

[10] M. Russell Ballard, "Strength in Counsel," *Ensign,* November 1993, and Robert D. Hales, "Strengthening Families: Our Sacred Duty," *Ensign,* May 1999.

[11] D&C 132:65 and Genesis 16:1–3.

Antagonists accused the church of giving the first wife no real choice in the practice of polygamy—implying that she had no power to stop the practice.[12] However, like all of the Lord's commandments, there is only the capacity to obey or disobey the law. The consultation verse 61 requires of the husband does not give the first wife the authority to enforce a monogamous marriage (which is evidenced by the command to both men and women in verses 3–6), but rather an opportunity to raise and address concerns. Once addressed, all parties involved should give their consent for the marriage to proceed, because that is the requirement of the law.

The law of Sarah provides for the possibility that the first wife may refuse to abide by the law of plural marriage. If, after learning about the law (verse 64) and counseling with her husband concerning a specific new wife (verse 61),[13] a first wife simply refuses the new marriage, then the church has the authority to override her decision and authorize the marriage, exempting the man from the law of Sarah and relieving him of his wife's disobedience (verse 65). In other words, if both husband and wife are commanded to live

---

[12] For an example, see "Polygyny in the Mormon Movement: The Law of Abraham and the Law of Sarah," Ontario Consultants on Religious Tolerance, www.ReligiousTolerance.org/lds_poly3.htm. The portion of this document relating to the law of Sarah is replicated in many places on the Internet without citation to an original source. See also Jim Day, "Joseph Smith's Many Wives," www.TrialsOfAscension.net/mormon.html, and many others.

[13] Verse 61 uses the term "virgin," which includes previously married women who were not guilty of adultery. See 1 Samuel 25:39 and Joel 1:8.

the law, and the wife will not accede, it should not prevent her spouse from complying with the Lord's commandment.

Members of the LDS Church believe that an individual is responsible only for his or her own sins and not for the sins of others.[14] Without the release from the law of Sarah permitted by the Lord in verse 65, a man would be guilty of violating his agreement to live in a polygamous marriage (verses 3–6) because of the disobedience of his first wife. This would violate the precept taught in the second Article of Faith, which is why the church has the authority to override the first wife's choice to withhold her consent and exempt the man from the law of Sarah.[15]

While the implications and requirements of the law of celestial marriage might seem egregious and demeaning to some and exalting to others, its purpose is clearly defined in verse 63 of Section 132. The law was given so that members of the early Mormon Church could "multiply and replenish the earth . . . for their exaltation in the eternal worlds, that they may bear the souls of men," all of which they felt would glorify God.[16]

---

[14] D&C, Articles of Faith 1:2.

[15] See page 153 no. 3.

[16] D&C 132:63.

The revelation contained in Section 132 and the practice of polygamy became an immediate problem for Joseph and the church. Because of the monogamous tradition of the society in which Joseph lived, it was simple for people to make accusations of adultery, lasciviousness, and sexual perversion against the Prophet and others who had been commanded to live the law. Perversion of the law by such men as John C. Bennett, and others who were out seeking to sate their sexual appetites, resulted in the seduction of innocent women and added fuel to the fire of controversy surrounding the practice. Also, misunderstanding of the law by some members of the church—men and women—unwittingly aided the church's enemies.

This uproar over polygamy—which continues today to some degree—eventually contributed to the deaths of Joseph and Hyrum Smith in Carthage Jail. It was also a significant factor in the expulsion of the Saints from Kirtland, Ohio; the state of Missouri; and Nauvoo, Illinois. It ultimately initiated a persistent legal battle against the LDS Church by the U.S. Government with the intent of either stopping the practice of plural marriage or destroying the church altogether.

Chapter Seven _____
Congress Attacks Polygamy

Although the Government of the United States took an aggressive stance against polygamy from its inception, Brigham Young's 1852 endorsement of the doctrine of multiple wives and the actual practice of polygamy accelerated the fight against the church.

The goal of the Republican Party platform in 1856 was to eradicate polygamy and slavery, what the Republicans described as the "twin relics of barbarism."[1] The southern states seceded after the election of Abraham Lincoln in 1860, which thrust slavery into the forefront of the nation's consciousness. Thereafter, the Republican Party dominated Congress throughout the balance of the nineteenth century. By the end of the Civil War, the problem of slavery had been momentarily resolved and the Republicans turned their sights on the other "twin"—polygamy. However, the intention of the fight that ensued was not to destroy the practice of polygamy by itself, but to destroy the "Mormon re-

_____
[1] *Congressional Globe* (Washington, D.C.; Government Printing Office, 1860), 1410.

ligion" in its entirety, as will be discussed throughout this chapter. This strong anti-Mormon sentiment was expressed by Senator John T. Morgan of Alabama in 1886 when he commented on the church's use of the First Amendment to defend its religious practices:

> In dealing with this corporation or with its associated ecclesiastical organization I do not feel that I am dealing with a religious establishment. I feel that I am dealing with something that is entirely irreligious, that has no just pretension at all to be called a religion in a Christian country. It would be a very fair religion in China or in any Mohammedan country; it would do very well for the Congo Free State perhaps; but in Christian America this can hardly be rated as an establishment of religion.[2]

Although polygamy was abhorrent in the eyes of those who opposed it on moral grounds, it was so interrelated with the church itself and its very existence that "attempts to stamp out polygamy almost inexorably became attacks on the institution of the Mormon Church and Mormons in general."[3] After a visit to Utah, President Rutherford B. Hayes informed Congress that polygamy could "only be suppressed by taking away the political

---

[2] *Congressional Record* 17:509.

[3] Zion 1988, 159.

power of the sect which encourages and sustains it."[4] Government leaders of the late 1800s quickly concluded that the only way to control the LDS Church was to destroy it.

The Morrill Anti-bigamy Act of 1862

When President Lincoln was asked by T.B.H. Stenhouse what course he intended to pursue with regards to the Mormons, it was reported that he replied with one of his famous homilies:

> Stenhouse, when I was a boy on the farm in Illinois there was a great deal of timber on the farms which we had to clear away. Occasionally we would come to a log which had fallen down. It was too hard to split, too wet to burn, and too heavy to move, so we plowed around it. That's what I intend to do with the Mormons. You go back and tell Brigham Young that if he will let me alone I will let him alone.[5]

However, Congress had no intention of leaving the Mormons alone. Anti-bigamy laws had been in existence for hundreds of years in Western Europe, and eventually in the United States. From the day Joseph Smith started marrying multiple wives, the church was living in defiance of existing state laws.

---

[4] Richardson 1896–99, 7:606.

[5] Larson 1971, 60.

However, the first formal attempt to eliminate the practice of polygamy came in 1856. Representative Justin Smith Morrill of Vermont introduced an act that would outlaw polygamy (termed "bigamy" in the act). Because of the problems that eventually led to the Civil War, the act was not taken up by Congress for six years; however, in 1862 the Morrill Anti-Bigamy Act finally became law.[6] The Act had three sections:

1. The first section prohibited any person with either a living husband or wife from marrying any other person, whether married or single, in a territory of the United States. This was defined as "bigamy."

   a. As punishment, a fine of up to $500 and up to five years in prison was imposed.

   b. Those individuals who had been legally divorced, had annulments, or had remarried after their spouse had been missing for five years or more were excepted.

2. The second section revoked the 1855 Incorporation Act of the Utah Territorial Legislature (which had incorporated The Church of Jesus Christ of Latter-day Saints) and all other acts that had anything to do with polygamy.

3. The third section prohibited any religious or

---

[6] Statutes 1879, 12:501.

charitable organization in any territory from acquiring or holding any real estate valued at more than $50,000. All real estate in excess of that value would escheat to the United States.

a.   Property acquired prior to the Act was exempt.

The following published comments exemplify the historical fervor of the anti-polygamists and the anti-Mormons who had instigated the Morrill Anti-Bigamy Act. (All references to "Territory" or "Territorial" refer to the Utah Territory.)

The young people are familiarized to indecent exposures of all kinds; the Mormons call their wives their cattle; they choose them pretty much as they choose their cattle . . . Young calls his women his cows.[7, 8]
– *John Cradlebaugh*
Associate Justice of the Territorial Supreme Court

I do not know that we could have looked for a different state of things in that Territory, considering the character of the people who have taken possession of it. We

---

[7] *Congressional Globe* 1860, Appendix, 194.

[8] There is no documentary evidence that Brigham Young ever referred to his wives as "cows." Mr. Cradlebaugh's reference may have stemmed from the book, *Utah and the Mormons,* by Benjamin G. Ferris, (Harper and Brothers, 1854), or from an article published by the *New York Times* when it reviewed the book ("The Mormons in Utah," 30 June 1854), both of which refer to male Mormons treating women and their wives like cattle.

certainly had no right to expect from them
a very high degree of morality.[9]
                        – *John S. Millson*
                        U.S. Representative for Virginia

It is not true that polygamy pretends to any
religious sanction. It is not true that the
Mormons practice it as a pious observance.
. . . Plainly, then, it is an unsound argument and a pernicious philosophy which
conduces to such absurd and mischievous
consequences.[10]
                        – *Roger A. Pryor*
                        U.S. Representative for Virginia

Ironically, the Morrill Act would not be used to
prosecute polygamists for twenty-two years. After
the Act was passed, the government accomplished
nothing of importance against polygamy or the
leadership of the church until 1871 when James B.
McKean was appointed the new federal judge in
Utah territory. He was "rabidly anti-Mormon and
determined to enforce the national policy against
polygamy despite all opposition."[11]

Under Judge McKean's leadership, Thomas
Hawkins became the first to be indicted for having more than one wife, but not under the Morrill Act. Rather, he was convicted under an 1851

---

[9] *Congressional Globe* 1860, 1492.

[10] *Congressional Globe* 1860, 1496.

[11] Zion 1988, 137.

Utah statute for adulterous relations, fined $500, and sentenced to three years at hard labor. Immediately thereafter, Brigham Young and other church leaders were indicted under a Utah statute against lewd and lascivious relations. Despite the apparent impotence of the Morrill Act, Judge McKean was determined to eradicate polygamy and the LDS Church. Evidence of the real intent of the anti-polygamy prosecutions was expressed by Judge McKean during the trial of Brigham Young when he said:

> It is . . . proper to say that while the case at bar is called *The People versus Brigham Young,* its other and real title is *Federal Authority versus Polygamic Theocracy* . . . The one government arrests the other in the person of its chief, and arraigns it at his bar. *A system is on trial in the person of Brigham Young.* Let all concerned keep this fact steadily in view; and let that government rule without a rival which shall prove to be in the right.[12]

Thomas Hawkins' conviction and the indictments of Brigham Young and others were later dismissed when in 1872, the Supreme Court declared that the indictment juries were improperly impaneled.

Although the Morrill Anti-Bigamy Act was de-

---

[12] *Deseret News,* 18 October 1871. Emphasis added.

signed to strangle the practice of polygamy, punish those who practiced it, and destroy the church, as a practical matter it neither appointed officers to enforce it (which left enforcement in the hands of the Mormon-controlled legal system in Utah Territory) nor provided funds for its enforcement. Although multiple prosecutions were attempted, the Act was essentially unenforced until after the case of *Reynolds v. United States* in 1884.

The Poland Act of 1874

There was little sympathy for the Mormons prior to 1874 and they had few friends in Washington. The failure of the Morrill Act to curb the practice of polygamy only heated the desire of Congress to destroy the LDS Church's political authority.

In 1866, Senator Benjamin Wade of Ohio proposed a bill designed to finally destroy the power of the LDS Church. The bill would do the following:

1. Convert the Nauvoo Legion (which was still operating in Salt Lake City) to a territorial militia under the control of the federal governor.

2. Prohibit church officials from performing marriages.

3. Give the United States marshal the power to select all jurors.

4. Give the governor power to appoint county judges.

5. Put a tax on all real and personal church property valued in excess of $20,000.

6. Require the trustee-in-trust for the church to report under oath to the governor each year on all church financial operations.

The bill failed to pass, but many of its features were incorporated into a bill by Senator Abram H. Cragin of New Hampshire in 1868. Additionally, his bill included a provision to abolish trial by jury in all cases under the Morrill Anti-Bigamy Act of 1862. This bill was withdrawn in favor of a bill by Representative Shelby M. Cullom of Illinois in 1869. The Cullom bill incorporated most of the provisions of Senator Cragin's bill, but declared cohabitation a misdemeanor and included provisions to deprive plural wives of immunity as witnesses in cases involving their husbands. It also allowed the president to send U.S. Army troops into Utah and raise a 25,000 man militia in the territory to enforce the law. One of its more egregious yet "compassionate" proposals was to confiscate all of the property of Mormons who were leaving the territory to evade prosecution. The property would be placed under "Gentile jurisdiction for the benefit of Mormon families." This bill passed the

House but failed in the Senate. Finally, a bill was proposed in 1869 by Congressman James Ashley of Ohio that would "dismember [Utah,] transferring large portions of the region to Nevada, Wyoming, and Colorado." This bill also failed to pass.[13]

Because the Mormons controlled the judiciary in the Utah Territory, enforcement of any Congressional legislation after the decisions in the Hawkins and Young matters proved almost impossible. Predictably, the next move by the federal government was directed against this judicial control. In President Ulysses S. Grant's message to Congress in 1873, he asked Congress to pass legislation that would ensure that the judicial system in Utah was no longer controlled by LDS Church members. He further noted that he was "convinced that so long as Congress leaves the selection of jurors to the local authorities it will be futile to make any effort to enforce laws not acceptable to the majority of the people of the Territory, or which interfere with local prejudices or provide for the punishment of polygamy or any of its affiliated vices or crimes." In that same address, he enumerated other legal problems with the court system as authorized by the Territorial Legislature and dominated by church members.[14]

Shortly after these requests by President Grant, and in light of the antagonism against the church

[13] Campbell 1988, 324–326.

[14] Richardson 1896–99, 7:209–10.

that Congress had exhibited in preceding years, in 1874 Congress passed the Poland Act.[15] The Poland Act accomplished the following:

1. It nullified all earlier Supreme Court decisions favorable to the Mormons.

2. It created a new jury selection process which was primarily aimed at limiting Mormon control over the jurors that were selected for any given matter.

3. It stripped the territorial attorney and territorial marshal of most of their powers.

4. It restricted the jurisdiction of the probate courts in the territory (which had been given general jurisdiction over all legal conflicts) to the "commonly limited jurisdiction" over estates, wills, and normal probate matters. ("Commonly limited jurisdiction" means those areas of jurisdiction over which probate courts had historically governed.)

5. The Morrill Act had a three-year statute of limitations. Therefore, all any polygamous husband had to do was elude prosecution for three years and he would avoid the perils of indictment. The Saints found that the easiest method of accomplishing this was to send the husband on a three-year mission after he

---

[15] Statutes 1879, 18:253.

entered into a polygamous relationship.[16] The Poland Act eliminated the time constraint for enforcement of the statute.

Although the Poland Act paved the way for the federal government to prosecute polygamy under the Morrill Act, it did not solve one major problem: *proving* that a polygamous relationship or marriage existed. The conundrum that existed for government prosecutors was that if the first wife (or any one of the succeeding wives) was acknowledged by the husband as his legal wife, she could not testify against her husband because of the privileged testimony relationship between husbands and wives. Therefore, a wife's testimony was inadmissible under common law. If, however, the polygamous wife's relationship was not valid, as defined by federal law, then she could testify because she was not technically a wife. This would apply to any of the polygamist wives. However, Congress would not resolve this problem until later.

The Poland Act was the first effective federal law that would enforce the government's anti-polygamy and anti-Mormon bias. Consequently, when it became obvious to the church that it could no longer avoid prosecution, the church's leadership decided it was time to test the anti-polygamy acts.

---

[16] Zion 1988, 151.

Reynolds v. United States

George Reynolds was Brigham Young's private secretary. He was also a polygamist. In October of 1874, he was indicted under the Morrill Act for bigamy. It has always been asserted by LDS Church historians that the case was a test case to determine the constitutionality of the Morrill Act because Reynolds agreed to cooperate with his prosecutors and have his second wife, Amelia Jane Schofield, testify in return for the government's agreement to not seek a harsh punishment. He was asked to be the guinea pig in this matter by George Q. Cannon of the First Presidency. Consequently, Reynolds was convicted of polygamy because of Amelia Jane's testimony.[17]

After his conviction, Reynolds appealed to the Utah Supreme Court on the grounds that his indictment was improper due to the fact that the grand jury was composed of twenty-three members in accordance with the requirement of the Poland Act, not the fifteen members required under the Utah statute. The Utah Supreme Court agreed and reversed the conviction. Although this was an initial victory for Reynolds, it left him vulnerable to a second indictment because of the sworn testimony of his polygamous wife. His marriage to her was now a matter of public record. Subsequently, in October of 1875 a second indictment against him was handed down

---

[17] Roberts 1930, 5:469.

that complied with the Utah statute for grand jury indictments.

Because a conviction was guaranteed if Amanda testified, she went into hiding. However, the court ruled that because her testimony in the previous trial was under oath and since she could not be found, her prior testimony could be entered into evidence. So Reynolds was convicted a second time. He was fined $500 and sentenced to two years in prison at hard labor. An appeal was made to the Utah Supreme Court, but that court upheld the conviction.[18] The only avenue of appeal remaining was to the United States Supreme Court.

Upon hearing all the arguments of the *Reynolds* case, the U.S. Supreme Court ruled that although the First Amendment protected belief, it did not protect conduct as pertaining to religion, and that "polygamy has always been odious among the northern and western nations of Europe" and therefore was an offence at common law, and "subversive of good order."[19]

The decision was ill received in Utah. The church believed the Constitution to be divinely inspired[20] and was relying on the First Amendment to protect it against anti-polygamy and other egregious laws that had been passed, and others that

[18] 1 Utah 319 (1876).

[19] 98 U.S. 164–165.

[20] D&C 1981, 101:79–80.

were sure to follow. Brigham Young had previously taught that "[t]here is not a single constitution of any single state, much less the constitution of the Federal Government, that hinders a man from having two wives; and I defy all the lawyers of the United States to prove the contrary."[21] But the Supreme Court had decided otherwise. Although this decision was a severe blow to the church's doctrine and beliefs, its immediate impact was limited since the *Reynolds* case was unique and the basic problems of enforcing the Morrill Act remained.

The *Reynolds* case was tried in a charged environment since for decades (from 1820 to the *Reynolds* decision in 1878), the Mormons had endured persecution and prosecution. However, all three branches of government—Executive, Legislative, and Judicial—were determined to eradicate not only polygamy, but the Mormon Church itself. Since its ruling, *Reynolds* has been the precedent that the court has relied upon in all polygamy cases. Precedent is a powerful, iron-clad ruler, but as shall be seen, chinks are developing in that armor.[22]

The Edmunds Act of 1882
In 1882, Congress passed the Edmunds Act.[23]

[21] JD 1967, 1:365.

[22] See Chapter Ten.

[23] Statutes 1879, 22:30.

The bill was sponsored by Senator George F. Edmunds, a Republican from Vermont and its declared purpose was to correct the problems of the Morrill Act. It contained the following provisions:

1. Polygamy replaced bigamy as a criminal offense.

2. Men who simultaneously married two or more women would be convicted of polygamy, in addition to the prohibition of the Morrill Act.

3. Cohabitation (living with more than one woman at the same time) became an offense, thereby eliminating the need for proof of marriage.

4. Cohabiting was a misdemeanor punishable by a fine of up to $300 or six months in jail or both.

5. Polygamy and cohabitation were allowed to be charged in the same indictment.

6. Jurors were disqualified for having or believing in multiple wives. This not only eliminated jurors who were polygamists, but jurors who were sympathetic to the practice.

7. Utah registration and election offices held by Mormons were vacated and provision made for their replacement.

8. The right to vote or hold elective or appointed

public office was denied to polygamists and those involved in cohabitation.

9. A Utah Commission was created to oversee future elections and issue certificates to those lawfully elected. The Utah Commission introduced the requirement of a "test oath" for women supporting and adhering to the anti-polygamy laws, which was expanded to all voters after the Edmunds-Tucker Act.

The Edmunds Act not only simplified the judicial process of punishment which had been incorporated in the Morrill Act, but overcame the frustrations of that Act "by imposing massive civil punishments on the entire Mormon community." The underlying assumption of the Act was that "Mormonism should be eradicated." The "Edmunds Act was offered to Congress as a means of punishing Mormons."[24]

As a result of the enforcement of the Edmunds Act, many church leaders went underground—hiding from authorities that were relentless in the pursuit of prosecution. Additionally, the various Acts proscribed restrictions and automatic punishments for individuals without due process. This is known as a "bill of attainder," which is in direct violation of the Constitution. But none of this mattered to

---

[24] Zion 1988, 162–163, 165. It is interesting to note that no aspect of the anti-bigamy and anti-polygamy acts were ever overturned, meaning that a man living with (cohabiting with) two women in any of the U.S. territories today (Guam, Puerto Rico, etc.) are living illegally.

the congressmen who were again manifesting the old spirit of religious persecution that had been dogging the Mormons long before Section 132 of *The Doctrine and Covenants* was revealed.

The Edmunds-Tucker Act of 1887

Knowing that legal weaknesses such as the inability to force a polygamous wife to testify against her husband still existed, Senator Edmunds had attempted to strengthen the provisions of his 1882 Edmunds Act many times before Congress finally approved the Edmunds-Tucker Act of 1887. The purpose of the Act was clear: "Some provisions further tightened the polygamy laws. Others further restricted the civil freedoms of Mormons. A few were aimed directly at the church."[25] The Edmunds-Tucker Act contained the following provisions:

1. A wife could now testify against her husband in actions against bigamy, polygamy, or unlawful cohabitation, with some limited exceptions.

2. Witnesses could now be compelled to appear without a subpoena to prevent them from going into hiding.

3. Prosecution for adultery could be instituted the same way prosecution for other crimes was

---

[25] Zion 1988, 198.

instituted (via a grand jury or other means of indictment).

4. Every marriage was required to be certified by a certificate (a public record) that provided the date of the ceremony, the full names of the parties being married, and the officer officiating at the ceremony.

5. The limitations of jurisdiction on the probate courts were continued.

6. Probate judges became presidential appointments rather than elected officials.

7. Illegitimate children (children born to marriages made illegal by this and previous Acts) born one year after the passage of the Act could not inherit.

8. The dower right of the wife to inherit one-third of her deceased husband's assets was reinstated, thus placing the first wife in the preeminent position for inheritance.

9. Women were disenfranchised. (The Territorial Legislature had previously allowed women the right to vote after Wyoming had given them that right.)

10. Secret ballots were allowed.

11. The powers of the Utah Commission were reaffirmed.

12. A voter oath in support of the anti-polygamy laws was instituted.

13. Control of public education was placed in the hands of federal officials.

14. The territorial militia (the Nauvoo Legion) was abolished.

15. Disincorporation of the church was reaffirmed and the attorney general was instructed to complete the disincorporation required under the Morrill Act.

16. The Perpetual Emigrating Fund Company was dissolved and the territorial legislature was prohibited from enacting any law that would bring people into the territory for any purpose.

The Edmunds-Tucker Act was designed to dismantle the LDS Church, destroy its political power and influence in U.S. territories, and force members of the church to adhere to marital practices commonly accepted throughout the United States at that time. President Chester Author had recommended these drastic measures in an effort to assume "absolute political control of the Territory of Utah."[26] His successor, President Grover Cleveland, urged Congress the next year to allow no further emigration of Mormons into the coun-

---

[26] Richardson 1896–99, 8:250.

try.[27] When compared to modern civil liberties, the prosecutions that occurred immediately after the Edmunds-Tucker Act was enacted clearly stepped "over the line to become persecution, [and signaled] clearly that it was Mormonism itself, not just polygamy, that the federal government wished to eradicate."[28]

Over thirty years of legislation had finally created laws that could destroy the LDS Church and harm its members due to its belief in and practice of polygamy. The various acts could take away both church and private property. They reversed all territorial legislation pertaining to the church, effectively disincorporating (dissolving) the church. They allowed for imprisonment of practicing members without due process. An issue of civil rights of this magnitude would not be seen again in the United States until the race riots of the early 1960s. The *Reynolds* case proved the federal government's iron will concerning the matter, but the church attempted one last appeal. On May 19, 1890, the United States Supreme Court heard the appeal on the case of the *Mormon Church v. United States, Late Corporation of the Church of Jesus Christ of Latter-day Saints, et al. v. United States, Romney v. Same*, 136 U.S. 1 (1890). The Court affirmed the constitutionality of the Edmunds-Tucker Act and the actions that dissolved the church and escheated its property. There

---

[27] Richardson 1896–99, 8:362.

[28] Zion 1988, 209.

was no other legal recourse available to the church. Polygamy had to go if the church was to survive.

It is interesting to note that all of the anti-polygamy acts were enforceable only in the territories of the United States—not in the states themselves. Should the Territory of Utah become a state, the state would have authority to reinstate the practice of polygamy (authority guaranteed the state by the Constitution). It is therefore not surprising that when Utah petitioned to become a state six years later, Congress required a prohibition against polygamy in its constitution, thereby closing the only remaining legal loophole the LDS Church could use to protect the practice of polygamy.[29] The requirement was enacted in the Utah Constitution as follows:

Article 3 – Ordinance
The following ordinance shall be irrevocable without the consent of the United States and the people of this State: [Religious toleration — Polygamy forbidden.]

First: — Perfect toleration of religious sentiment is guaranteed. No inhabitant of this State shall ever be molested in person or property on account of his or her mode of religious worship; but polygamous or plural marriages are forever prohibited.

---

[29] Utah Enabling Act, 28 U.S. Statutes at Large 108.

The same requirement was placed in the constitutions of Arizona,[30] New Mexico,[31] and Oklahoma.[32] These provisions are still in the constitutions of these states.

This Article was extremely severe since it was "irrevocable without the consent of the United States and the people of said State." In a Supreme Court case decided one hundred years later that was not directly associated with polygamy, Justice Scalia (with whom Chief Justice William Rehnquist and Justice Thomas joined) reviewed these prohibitions and in a dissenting opinion stated that this prohibition was so severe that not only were "each of [the] parts" of these States not "open on impartial terms" to polygamists, but even the States as a whole were not; polygamists would have to persuade the whole country to their way of thinking.[33] Justice Scalia obviously recognized the severity of this punishment against the Mormon people, a severity that has only been equaled by the United States' prohibition against drug use in religious practices by the Native Americans, which has since been rescinded.

Idaho adopted such a prohibition in its constitution on its own, which was approved when the 51st Congress passed its Act of Admission of

---

[30] Arizona Enabling Act, 36 U.S. Statutes at Large 569.

[31] New Mexico Enabling Act, 36 U.S. Statutes at Large 558.

[32] Oklahoma Enabling Act, 34 U.S. Statutes at Large 269.

[33] *Romer, Governor of Colorado, et al. v. Evans et al.*, 517 U.S. 620, 94-1039 (1996).

Idaho.[34] The Idaho Legislature had also passed a strict prohibition act against polygamists (and those who taught or believed in, or belonged to an organization that taught or believed in polygamy) that among other things, restricted them from voting:

[N]o person . . . who is a bigamist or polygamist or who teaches, advises, counsels, or encourages any person or persons to become bigamists or polygamists, or to commit any other crime defined by law, or to enter into what is known as plural or celestial marriage, or who is a member of any order, organization or association which teaches, advises, counsels, or encourages its members or devotees or any other persons to commit the crime of bigamy or polygamy, or any other crime defined by law . . . is permitted to vote at any election, or to hold any position or office of honor, trust, or profit within this Territory.[35]

This statute even denied polygamists the right to make polygamy legal under any circumstances because it deprived them of the right to vote. The provision was upheld by the Supreme Court. Justice Field wrote the unanimous opinion wherein he

---

[34] 26 U.S. Statutes at Large 215.

[35] Section 501 of the Revised Statutes of Idaho Territory.

stated that the statute was not open to any "constitutional or legal objection."[36]

It is clear that the government of the United States was adamantly opposed to polygamy and to the teachings of the Church of Jesus Christ of Latter-day Saints. All branches of the government—Legislative, Judicial, and Executive (including bureaucratic government agencies)—participated in this legal persecution, going far beyond the abolition of what they considered a moral issue or the preservation of the traditional monogamist marital relationship. It denied individual members of the LDS Church of many of their civil rights, and the church itself of its very existence. It is worth noting again that the very laws that were declared constitutional prohibiting polygamy under the mass hysteria of religious persecution against the Mormons in the nineteenth century would, in all probability, be declared unconstitutional today as bills of attainder—the civil punishment of individuals (in this case members of the Church of Jesus Christ of Latter-day Saints) without due process of law.[37]

However, the result of the thirty-eight-year struggle between the LDS Church and the federal government was the church's decision to abandon the practice of—but not the belief in—polygamy. The church officially discontinued the practice with the Manifesto of 1890.

---

[36] *Davis v. Beason,* 133 U.S. 333, 346–347 (1890).

[37] U.S. Constitution, Article 1, Section 9, Paragraph 3.

Chapter Eight _____
The Manifestos

The Manifesto of 1890

The Edmunds Act of 1882 created the Utah Commission, which was mandated (among other things) to regularly report on the Mormon practice of polygamy to the federal government. This commission reported in August 1890 that polygamous marriages were still being performed in the Endowment House (a building created to host marriage ceremonies until the completion of the Salt Lake Temple). This report, combined with the unfavorable ruling from the U.S. Supreme Court the previous May and the realization that the church would not survive if it continued the practice of polygamy, brought about what members of the LDS Church believe was the prophetically inspired decision to discontinue the practice. On Sunday, October 6, 1890, the following declaration (recorded as Official Declaration—1 in *The Doctrine and Covenants*) was read at a session of the LDS Church's General Conference in Salt Lake City, Utah:

To Whom It May Concern:
Press dispatches having been sent for political purposes, from Salt Lake City, which have been widely published, to the effect that the Utah Commission, in their recent report to the Secretary of the Interior, allege that plural marriages are still being solemnized and that forty or more such marriages have been contracted in Utah since last June or during the past year, also that in public discourses the leaders of the Church have taught, encouraged and urged the continuance of the practice of polygamy—

I, therefore, as President of the Church of Jesus Christ of Latter-day Saints, do hereby, in the most solemn manner, declare that these charges are false. We are not teaching polygamy or plural marriage, nor permitting any person to enter into its practice, and I deny that either forty or any other number of plural marriages have during that period been solemnized in our Temples or in any other place in the Territory.

One case has been reported, in which the parties allege that the marriage was performed in the Endowment House, in Salt Lake City, in the Spring of 1889, but I have not been able to learn who performed the ceremony; whatever was done in this matter was without my knowledge. In consequence of this alleged occurrence the Endowment House was, by my instructions, taken down without delay.

Inasmuch as laws have been enacted by Congress forbidding plural marriages, which laws have been pronounced constitutional by the court of last resort, I hereby declare my intention to submit to those laws, and to use my influence with the members of the Church over which I preside to have them do likewise.

There is nothing in my teachings to the Church or in those of my associates, during the time specified, which can be reasonably construed to inculcate or encourage polygamy; and when any Elder of the Church has used language which appeared to convey any such teaching, he has been promptly reproved. And I now publicly declare that my advice to the Latter-day Saints is to refrain from contracting any marriage forbidden by the law of the land.

Wilford Woodruff
President of the Church of Jesus Christ of Latter-day Saints

President Lorenzo Snow offered the following:

I move that, recognizing Wilford Woodruff as the President of the Church of Jesus
Christ of Latter-day Saints, and the only
man on the earth at the present time who
holds the keys of the sealing ordinances,
we consider him fully authorized by virtue of his position to issue the Manifesto
which has been read in our hearing, and
which is dated September 24th, 1890, and
that as the Church in General Conference
assembled, we accept his declaration concerning plural marriages as authoritative
and binding.
    The vote to sustain the foregoing mo-
tion was unanimous.
    Salt Lake City, Utah, October 6, 1890.[1]

Unlike many of the revelations contained within *The Doctrine and Covenants* which begin by
announcing that the revelation is from the Lord,
the Manifesto begins with the declaration, "To
Whom It May Concern." Throughout the history
of the LDS Church, announcements and procla-
mations directed primarily to people other than
church members have avoided phrases similar to
"Thus Saith the Lord." Though certainly directed
to church members, the declaration's main audi-

---

[1] See D&C 1981, Official Declaration—1 and Excerpts.

ence was the Utah Commission, the federal government, and the world. Despite the unusual introduction, members of the LDS Church believe the declaration to be the result of revelation from the Lord.

The first, second, and third paragraphs of the Manifesto reflect the comments in the Utah Commission Report to the Secretary of the Interior dated August 22, 1890. In that report, the Commission stated that it believed forty-one persons had entered into polygamous relationships since their last report and that the practice was still being taught by the church (however, no evidence was presented by the commission to substantiate its claim). President Woodruff declared these charges to be false and immediately dismantled the Endowment House to emphasize his conviction.

In the fifth and last paragraph, President Woodruff denied that he had taught or encouraged the teaching of polygamy to church members "during the time specified" (referring back to the Utah Commission's reporting period), and that those who had been discovered doing so were reprimanded. Then President Woodruff advised the members of the church to refrain from entering into any marriage that was contrary to the laws of the United States.

The forth paragraph outlines the reasons thta the church should cease the practice of polygamy:

- Congress passed laws forbidding the practice of polygamy.

- Those laws were pronounced constitutional by the highest court in the land.

The Manifesto does not renounce polygamy, just the practice of it at that time. There would not be—nor could there be—a repudiation and denial of the revelation given to Joseph Smith as recorded in Section 132 of *The Doctrine and Covenants* without undermining church members' belief in prophets and divine revelation. President Woodruff merely submitted to the laws of the land by forbidding the practice of polygamy, and used his influence to convince the Saints to do the same.

Was the church justified in ceasing that portion of the revelation concerning the practice of polygamy (albeit reluctantly)? Yes! When the Lord commanded the Saints to build a temple in Jackson County, Missouri, and the Saints were unable to comply due to persecution, the Lord responded with the following instruction found in Section 124 of *The Doctrine and Covenants*:

Verily, verily, I say unto you, that when I give a commandment to any of the sons of men to do a work unto my name, and those sons of men go with all their might and with all they have to perform that work, and cease not their diligence, and their enemies come upon them and hinder them from performing that work, behold, it behooveth me to require that work no more at the hands of those sons of men, but to accept of their offerings.[2]

This instruction was relied upon again when the Saints were unable to redeem Zion (Independence and Jackson County, Missouri) due to the persecution created by Governor Lilburn W. Boggs' infamous Extermination Order. However, whether Wilford Woodruff's declaration was the result of a revelation or merely a decision on the part of the church's leading councils makes no difference—the decision to discontinue the practice of polygamy was supported by the revealed word of the Lord.

Mormons believe there is no question that the Lord revealed the law of celestial marriage found in Section 132 and commanded, "all those who have this law revealed unto them must obey the same."[3] The Saints complied with this commandment to the extent that many of the church's leaders had to go into hiding or on missions or be confined in jail rather than disobey the Lord. However, the enemies of the church did everything in

[2] D&C 1981, 124:45–55 (verse quoted: 49).

[3] D&C 1981, 132:3.

their power to hinder that obedience. Law after law was passed prohibiting first bigamy, then polygamy, and finally cohabitation. The federal government even attempted to disenfranchisement the church to ensure that polygamy would be stopped and those who lived it punished.

Through all of this, the Saints were attempting to live what they considered God's law and pursued every legal avenue available to challenge the statutory law of the land. Finally, after 25 years of congressional and legal battles, the Supreme Court validated the Morrill Act and the Lord, through His authorized prophet, Wilford Woodruff, suspended the practice of polygamy. Per the requirements of Section 124, He was satisfied that the Saints had done all in their power to comply with His directives, so He revealed the Manifesto.

But the Manifesto did not destroy the new and everlasting covenant of marriage, nor the *belief* in the plurality of wives. The law remained, but the practice of polygamy—like the redemption of Zion and the building of the temple in Jackson County, Missouri—was stopped for a season, with the following exceptions:

Matthias Foss Cowley, 1858–1940, a member of the Quorum of Twelve, objected to the Manifesto and continued practicing polygamy. He was ordained an Apostle on October 7, 1897, and resigned from the Quorum on October 28, 1905.

His priesthood was suspended as a disciplinary action on May 11, 1911, but he was never excommunicated or disfellowshipped and remained an Apostle. However, he was never reinstated to the Quorum. His priesthood was finally restored on April 3, 1936.

John Whittaker Taylor, 1858–1916, was ordained an Apostle on May 15, 1884. He resigned from the Quorum in April of 1905 and was excommunicated in 1911 because of continued disputes with church leadership. He was posthumously rebaptized by proxy and reinstated into the church in August of 1916 by two Stake Presidents. However, a year later the First Presidency officially stated that the reinstatement was null and void. He was officially rebaptized and reinstated under the direction of then LDS Church President David O. McKay in 1965.[4]

The Manifesto of 1904

It should be clearly understood that the Manifesto of 1890 did not succeed in totally abolishing polygamy. There were multiple members of the Church, including most of the general authorities, who were already living in polygamous relationships. These did not cease. It should also be clearly understood that the Manifesto did not de-

---

[4] Samuel W. Taylor, *Family Kingdom* (London: Hodder and Stroughton, 1951).

clare that the church was abandoning its belief in the doctrine of polygamy and eternal marriage. In fact, it could easily be argued that the Manifesto did not even restrict the practice at all (except for President Woodruff) because it merely "advised" the members to adhere to the laws of the land. No mention was made of the members living in polygamous relationships outside the United States, and the practice continued in Mexico and Canada for some time after the Manifesto was issued. It even continued on a limited basis in the United States. This condition continued for a period of fourteen years, whether authorized by church leaders or not. President Joseph F. Smith seemed to acknowledge the situation when he made the following declaration in General Conference on Wednesday, April 6, 1904:

> Now I am going to present a matter to you that is unusual and I do it because of a conviction which I feel that is the proper thing to do. I have taken the liberty of having written down [that] which I would like to have conveyed to your ears, that I may not be misunderstood or misquoted. I present this to the conference for your action.

At this point, President Smith read the following Official Statement, which amounted to a second Manifesto concerning plural marriage:

Inasmuch as there are numerous reports in circulation that plural marriages have been entered into contrary to the official declaration of President Woodruff, of September 26, 1890 commonly called the Manifesto, which was issued by President Woodruff and adopted by the Church at its General Conference, October, 6, 1890, which forbade any marriages volative [sic] of the law of the land; I Joseph F. Smith, President of the Church of Jesus Christ of Latter-day Saints, hereby affirm and declare that no such marriages have been solemnized with the sanction, consent or knowledge of the Church of Jesus Christ of Latter-day Saints, and I hereby announce that all such marriages are prohibited, and if any officer or member of the Church shall assume to solemnize or enter into any such marriage he will be deemed in transgression against the Church and will be liable to be dealt with, according to the rules and regulations thereof and excommunicated therefrom.

Joseph F. Smith
President of the Church of Jesus Christ of Latter-day Saints

President Francis M. Lyman, President of the

Quorum of Twelve presented the following resolution and moved for its adoption:

Resolved that we, the members of the
Church of Jesus Christ of Latter-day Saints,
in General Conference assembled, hereby
approve and endorse the statement and declaration of President Joseph F. Smith, just
made to this Conference concerning plural
marriages, and will support the courts of
the Church in the enforcement thereof.

The resolution was then adopted by unanimous
vote of the Conference.[5]

Although the presentation by President Smith
assumed that the original Manifesto "forbade any
marriages volative [sic] of the law of the land," the
language of that Manifesto did not so state. However, the Official Declaration of 1890 (which is
now a part of *The Doctrine and Covenants*) clearly
ended the practice of polygamy.[6] But members of
the LDS Church believe that it could not repudi-
ate the validity of the doctrine as revealed to Joseph Smith and recorded in Section 132 of *The
Doctrine and Covenants.*

---

[5] *Conference Reports,* The Church of Jesus Christ of Latter-day Saints, April 6, 1904,
p. 97. It should be noted that during the early years of the Church, at least one session
of General Conference was held on the 6th of both April and October, regardless of
what day of the week it fell on.

[6] On September 9, 1998, President Gordon B. Hinckley of the LDS Church on *Larry
King Live* made the following comment: "I condemn it, yes, as a practice, because I
think it [the *practice* of polygamy] is not doctrinal, it is not legal. And this church takes
the position that we will abide by the law."

It should be noted that neither the Manifesto of 1890 nor what has been called the second Manifesto of 1904 dealt with the problem of cohabitation. Nor does it appear that the government was interested in legally pursuing those still living in a polygamous relationship once the Manifesto was issued and Utah became a state. As a practical matter, polygamy continued to exist for a period of twenty or thirty years after the Manifesto, until those (either husbands or wives) who were living in polygamous relationships died. Once Utah became a state, the church property that had either been confiscated or placed in receivership was returned, and the church and the government settled into a state of mutual tolerance.

Chapter Nine _____
Politics and Polygamy

The Constitution of the United States provides for each state to have representation in Congress to ensure that their citizens are represented in the affairs of government. Congress is composed of the Senate and the House of Representatives. Each state is allowed two Senators, regardless of population, and the number of Representatives in the House is based on the state's population. Without these officials, citizens of the United States would be without political representation. Utah's population at the time of statehood only allowed the state one Representative.

As we have already seen, the federal government made a considerable effort between 1856 and 1890 to not only destroy the practice of polygamy in the Mormon Church, but to destroy the church itself. As a territory, Utah had applied for statehood several times without success—due to the stigma of polygamy. However, six years after the Manifesto of 1890 was published, Utah finally acquired statehood—on the condition that its constitution include a provision forever prohibiting polygamy. Although the government had successfully brought an end to the official practice of polygamy by the church, the negative emotion against both polygamy and the church continued in Washington's political arena. Two cases, one involving an elected member of the House of Representatives and the second an elected Senator, provide evidence of this discrimination.

Brigham Henry Roberts

B.H. Roberts (as he is usually referred to) was born March 13, 1857, in Warrington, Lancashire, England. His mother and father joined the church, but were later divorced. They had four children: Annie, Mary, Brigham, and Thomas. Brigham's mother, along with his sister Annie and baby Thomas, immigrated to the United States in 1865. Mary and Brigham were left behind in England, Mary with relatives and Brigham with a Mormon family named Tovey. However, in 1866, Brigham and his sister also immigrated to Utah and were reunited with their mother. The family settled in Davis County, Utah, where Brigham was baptized in 1867 by his stepfather. After serving several missions, Roberts was called to serve in the "First Council of Seventy" (First Quorum of Seventy).

B.H. Roberts was a polygamist and had fifteen children by two of his three wives. He married Sarah Louisa Smith in 1878. After bearing seven children, Sarah Louisa died on May 21, 1923. On October 2, 1884, Roberts married Celia Ann Dibble. She bore him eight children and died March 21, 1936. He married his third wife, Margaret Curtis Ship, in April of 1890. She had four children from a previous marriage and died March 13, 1926.

Roberts was arrested in December of 1886 for unlawful cohabitation. He had two wives at the time. He bonded in the amount of $1,000 for his court appearance, but upon consultation with church authorities, he left for England on a mission to avoid prosecution. When he returned from England he was called to the First Council of Seventy, but he remained in "retirement" (hiding) to avoid going to trial on his previous indictment. He finally surrendered himself to the authorities in April of 1889, and on May 1, 1889, he was sentenced to six months in prison and fined $200. He was released September 10, 1889, after serving his term. He married his third wife approximately six months later.

In 1895, Roberts was nominated on the Democratic ticket as Utah's Representative to Congress, but was defeated in the general election. He was again nominated in 1898 and won the election. He was to serve in the House of Representatives of the 56th Congress for the term running from

March 4, 1899 to March 3, 1901. At the time he was elected he was married to three women. When he went to be sworn in, his qualifications were immediately challenged because of his polygamous lifestyle and his seating was put on trial by the House Elections Committee. Further, he was prohibited from taking his seat in the House during his trial, which lasted for almost three quarters of what would have been his two-year term. When the committee finally voted, the decision was against seating him.

After the church issued the 1890 Manifesto, no particular effort was made by the government to dissolve existing polygamist unions, only to prevent future marriages. But Roberts was a polygamist, a fact that was uncontested, and with his election, it gave the government another opportunity to strike out at the church, using the practice of polygamy as the vanguard of its argument. Even though the church thought it had resolved the social implications of polygamy with the 1890 Manifesto, the political prejudice continued, with the result that Utah was left without representation in the House of Representatives for the 56th Congress. It also ended the political career of B.H. Roberts.

Brother Roberts remained a General Authority in the LDS Church for the rest of his life. He was a prolific writer. Perhaps his most famous work is the seven volume *History of the Church, Peri-*

od I, which he compiled and edited, and his own six volume *Comprehensive History of the Church.*[1] He died September 27, 1933.[2]

Reed Smoot

Reed Smoot was born January 10, 1862, in Salt Lake City, Utah. He married Alpha M. Eldredge in 1884. It was his only marriage. He did not participate in any polygamous relationships. He served two missions for the church and was called and sustained as an Apostle on April 8, 1900. He was a lifelong Utah Republican and was elected to the United States Senate in 1903.[3] On February 23, 1903, his credentials were presented to the U.S. Senate and immediately thereafter, Senator Julius C. Burrows of Michigan protested his seat. In his formal protest to the Committee on Privileges and Elections, Senator Burrows said:

[Reed Smoot] is one of a self-perpetuating body of fifteen men who, constituting the ruling authorities of the Church of Jesus Christ of Latter-day Saints, or "Mormon" Church, claim, and by their followers are accorded the right to claim, supreme au-

---

[1] See George Q. Cannon, ed., *Juvenile Instructor,* Vol. 34, p. 354 for a list of his writings.

[2] Compiled and adapted from the *LDS Biographical Encyclopedia.*

[3] The U.S. Constitution, Article 1, Section 3, provided for Senators to be elected by each state legislature. Amendment 17 to the Constitution (1913) changed that to election by popular vote.

thority . . . to shape the belief and control the conduct of those under them in all matters whatsoever, civil and religious, temporal and spiritual, and who thus . . . do so exercise the same as to inculcate and encourage a belief in polygamy and polygamous cohabitation.[4]

Senator Borrows' protest was preceded by a written protest to President Theodore Roosevelt and several members of the Senate from the Salt Lake Ministerial Association. In addition to the protests from the Ministerial Association and Senator Burrows, another protest was filed by Methodist Minister John Leilich, who added the charge that Senator Smoot was a polygamist.[5] However, unlike B. H. Roberts, Reed Smoot was allowed to take his seat in the Senate while the hearings proceeded before a committee of nine Republicans and five Democrats.

The two charges that could have disqualified him from taking his seat in the Senate were: (1) if he were a polygamist (because it violated the Edmunds-Tucker Act), and (2) if, as an Apostle, he advocated the doctrine of polygamy and gave allegiance to the church in all matters, superseding the laws of the government. However, it was not

---

[4] Senate Committee on Privileges and Elections, "In the Matter of the Protests Against the Right of Hon. Reed Smoot, a Senator from the State of Utah to Hold His Seat," 59th Congress, first session, Senate Document 486, Vol. 4932 (Washington: General Printing Office, 1970), 1.

[5] Shin 2005, 147.

primarily Reed Smoot that was on trial but the church itself. Senator Burrows had warned Smoot at the outset: "You are not on trial. It is the Mormon church that we intend to investigate, and we are going to see that those men obey the law."[6]

By the end of the committee hearings and the Senate trial, 3,482 petitions had been submitted to the Senate opposing Senator Smoot's seating. Members of the General Authorities of the Church had been subpoenaed to testify and several did, including President Joseph F. Smith. Some of his testimony placed the church in an unfavorable light. The church had issued the Manifesto in 1890, and statehood was conditioned upon the Utah State Constitution prohibiting polygamy in any form. Under oath, Chairman Burrows questioned President Smith concerning his marital status and his obedience to the current federal laws. President Smith answered: "Mr. Chairman, I have not claimed that in that case I have obeyed the law of the land. I do not claim so, and, as I said before, that I prefer to stand my chances against the law." He went on to state, "My friends . . . Gentiles and Jews and Mormons . . . all know that I have 5 wives."[7] Apostles Matthias Cowley and John Taylor, known polygamists and opponents to the Manifesto, were subpoenaed to testify but did

---

[6] Shin 2005, 159.

[7] 59th Congress, second session, *Congressional Record,* Vol. 41 (Washington: General Printing Office, 1907), 251.

not appear. Smoot, in the October General Conference of 1905, publicly refused to sustain either of them as members of the Twelve and as noted previously, they both resigned eventually from the Quorum.

On June 1, 1906, the committee voted to reject Reed Smoot as the Senator from Utah on a vote of seven to five. The matter then went to the full Senate where additional testimony was heard, including the petitions that had been before the committee and additional ones that were sent during the process. Various women's groups submitted petitions and the Reverend A.S. Bailey sent thousands of petitions from "Protestant evangelical congregations," stating that, "It is a theory of Mormonism that all power religious, business and political, belongs to the church."[8] However, President Roosevelt and the Republican party stood firmly behind Smoot and the final vote in the Senate on February 20, 1907, was 42 ayes to 28 nays, in Senator Smoot's favor. The Senator then continued to serve in the Senate for 29 years, from 1903 to 1932. Perhaps the only lasting memory of the affair was a jingle that appeared in the *San Francisco Call* newspaper on February 21, 1903:

---

[8] Shin 153, 155.

Can't you get wise to the fact, that you're
not wanted?
Don't you see that you wouldn't fit?
Back, pack your old carpet sack,
And spank your feet on the homeward track,
Scoot — Smoot — Scoot.

Senator Reed Smoot died in Saint Petersburg, Florida, in 1941.

The anti-polygamy and anti-Mormon fervor that seemingly had died down after the 1890 Manifesto and Utah's acceptance as a state was given resurgence with the election of B.H. Roberts. Perhaps his rejection by Congress should have been anticipated—even though he was the duly elected Representative from Utah—since he had been convicted by the Utah District Court under the anti-polygamy laws, and anti-polygamy fervor in Washington and the nation was still strong in 1899.

However, Reed Smoot's case was different. He was not a polygamist, yet his seat in the Senate was also challenged not because he practiced polygamy, but because he *believed* in polygamy and not only was he a Mormon, but an apostle—a member of the ruling body of the Mormon Church. The Committee eventually voted to deny seating Senator Smoot, but because of the influence of President

Theodore Roosevelt and other influential members of Congress, the Committee's vote was reversed and he was eventually permanently seated.

Apparently, the social stigma of polygamy continues even today. It is demonstrated by the rhetoric that is broadcast on the news every time a Mormon runs for national office. The presidential bid by Matt Romney illustrates this fact. He has faced much of the same criticism that was levied against B.H. Roberts and Senator Smoot in the early twentieth century. It is obvious that for some, hostility toward the LDS Church is still alive and well. Yet there are many members of the Church of Jesus Christ of Latter-day Saints who are currently serving as highly respected members of Congress, both as Representatives and as Senators, and it is unlikely that anyone would now challenge their ability to be sworn in on the basis of the church's continued belief in the doctrine of polygamy.

Chapter Ten _____

Polygamy Today

The Edmunds-Tucker Act, the *Reynolds* case, and the LDS Church Manifestos of 1890 and 1904 should have ended the story of polygamy—but it hasn't. The United States of America was created (among other reasons) to protect an individual's right to disagree: many people disagreed with the practice of polygamy; others disagreed with the Manifestos and the suspension of the practice. Individuals outside the LDS Church (many of whom left the church because of their belief in the now defunct practice) continued to participate in plural relationships after the two Manifestos eliminated the practice within The Church of Jesus Christ of Latter-day Saints. Whether it deserves it or not, however, the church has generally been associated with the issue every time it gains notoriety.

Polygamy has been practiced for millennia throughout the world and among many civilizations. At times it was considered legal and culturally acceptable. At other times it was considered immoral and unacceptable. Though few people practiced bigamy or polygamy during the early history of the United States, all states formed by the 1840s had anti-bigamy laws as a byproduct of Western Europe's position that polygamy was immoral. Polygamy only came to the forefront of the American psyche when it was introduced by Joseph Smith.

Primarily, only one organization endorsed polygamy at that time: The Church of Jesus Christ of Latter-day Saints. But many organizations— governmental and religious—rejected it. This began to change, however, with the death of Joseph Smith in June of 1844. Many groups broke away from the church at that time for many reasons, but two were significant because of their opposition to polygamy:[1]

• Sidney Rigdon was one of the principal LDS Church leaders during the period of the restoration. After Joseph's death, he claimed he had seen a vision in which he was told he should be appointed guardian of the church in order to "build it up to Joseph." The Saints rejected Sidney's claim and sustained the extant Twelve Apostles as the head of the Church.[2] Sidney

---

[1] After the Prophet was martyred, at least seventeen different individuals attempted to either form new churches or contend that they were authorized to succeed Joseph in leading the church he had organized in 1830. While several of these break offs are still active today, most were and continue to be small in number. The church Joseph restored, The Church of Jesus Christ of Latter-day Saints, has not only survived, but continues to grow. As of 2007, LDS Church membership stands in excess of 13 million.

[2] HC 1955, 7:231–242.

then left Nauvoo and returned to Pittsburgh,
Pennsylvania, where he began publishing a paper called the *Messenger and Advocate*. In his
paper, he denounced the Mormon Church and
the brethren in Nauvoo, charging them with
"spiritual wifery."[3] He was officially excommunicated from the church on September 8, 1844.
In April of 1845, he organized the Church of
Jesus Christ of the Children of Zion and proclaimed himself president. Little came of his
movement.[4] He died in obscurity in Allegh-
eny County, New York, in 1876.

• Joseph Smith III, the Prophet's son, was introduced at a conference of the Reorganized
Church of Jesus Christ of Latter Day Saints
(RLDS) held on April 6, 1860, (16 years after Joseph Smith was martyred). He accepted his calling as president in succession to his
father Joseph Smith, Jr., and was sustained as
president of the RLDS Church. The church
was organized based on two fundamental dis-
agreements with the original LDS Church:
leadership (RLDS Church members believed
the presidency should be patriarchal—father
to son) and polygamy. Today, this church is
known as the Community of Christ. It has
become the largest of the successionist move-

---

[3] *Messenger and Advocate*, 15 March 1845, 1:176.

[4] RHC 1911, 3:9–12.

ments from the Mormon Church. In recent years, it built a temple on its property in Independence, Missouri, dedicated to the pursuit of peace. At the present time, it has approximately 250,000 members throughout the world. It is organized with apostles, seventies, high priests, elders, priests, teachers, and deacons. Women are allowed to hold the priesthood, and as of this writing, one is currently a member of the presidents of seventy and one is serving as an apostle.

There were at least seventeen splinter groups that broke from the main body of the Mormon Church after the death of Joseph Smith. Most of these groups either failed to survive more than a few years, or joined with some of the larger groups that have survived to this date, the most prominent of these being the Community of Christ.

The next notable breaks from the LDS Church came after the Manifesto of 1890 was published. These splinter groups left because they felt the church had abandoned the revelation given to Joseph Smith in Section 132 of *The Doctrine and Covenants*. There were at least seven groups that eventually organized their own churches: The Church of the First Born of the Fullness of Times; The Church of the Lamb of God; Apostolic United Brethren; The Fundamentalist Church of Jesus Christ of Latter-Day Saints; Latter day Church of Christ; The True and Living Church of Jesus Christ of the Last Days; and The Church of Jesus Christ in Solemn Assembly, which was formed by Alexander Joseph in 1974 after he left the Apostolic United Brethren. All but one of these (The True and Living Church of Jesus Christ of the Last Days, founded by James Harmson in Manti, Utah, and organized May 3, 1994) were eventual derivatives from the claims made by Lorin C. Woolley in the early 1930s. Woolley claimed that on the evening of September 27, 1886, John Taylor, President of the Church of Jesus Christ of Latter-day Saints, while staying at the Woolley home in Centerville, Utah, received a spirit visitation from Joseph Smith, Jr., the church's founder. He further claimed that during this visit, Joseph Smith directed John Taylor to preserve the practice of polygamy and after the supposed vision closed, John Taylor required each of the men in the room to promise to continue the practice of polygamy. The Mormon Church has always stated that no such "revelation" exists in the historical records of the church kept while John Taylor was president, and from the diaries and other records from the period, researchers cannot place John Taylor in Centerville, Utah, at that time. Most of these churches still adhere to the major doctrines of the LDS Church and all of them believe in *The Book of Mormon*. Their principal explanation for breaking away from the church remains the open practice of polygamy. However, since the issuance of the second Manifesto in 1904, it has always been the policy of the LDS Church to excommunicate any member of the church found practicing or advocating the practice of polygamy.

Non-LDS Polygamy

There is another group that requires notice here because of its dedication to the decriminalization of polygamy. Its name is TruthBearer.org, or Organization for Christian Polygamy. This group is not affiliated in any way with the Mormon Church and is not a derivative of any break off from the Mormon Church. At its website there is a specific disclaimer incased in a box that reads:

> This is NOT about polyandry or polyamory.
> This is NOT about fornication or adultery.
> This is NOT about group marriage or wife swapping.
> This is NOT about dishonest bigamy or infidelity.
> This is NOT about underaged or arranged marriage.
> This is NOT about any form of Mormonism.
> This is NOT about redefining marriage.

The declared mission of this group is "Bringing Christian Polygamy to the Churches."

This is a fundamentalist, non-sectarian Christian movement founded by Mark Henkel and is located in Old Orchard Beach, Maine. The group has attempted to convince fundamentalist Christians and the ministers and pastors of fundamentalist Christian churches that polygamy is an acceptable doctrine of the Christian faith. In Mr. Henkel's words, "Polygamy rights is the next civil-rights battle." His argument, as written by Elise Soukup of *Newsweek* magazine, is that "if Heather can have two mommies, she should also be able to have two mommies and a daddy."[5] Mr. Henkel has appeared all over the United States, on multiple news and talk shows, and in some foreign countries. His principal proposal is the decriminalization of—and the open practice of—polygamy.

In Ms. Soukup's March 20, 2006 *Newsweek* article, "Polygamists, Unite!" she also notes that, "[e]xperts estimate that there are between 30,000 and 50,000 polygamists in the United States who practice a form of Mormonism, though the Church of Jesus Christ of Latter-day Saints, most commonly associated with the term 'Mormon,' banned the practice in 1890 . . . There's also a growing number of evangelical Christian and Muslim polygamists—some experts say they may even exceed the number."

Just how successful Mr. Henkel will be in his personal crusade is not known. However, it is evident from a review of his interviews and articles (which appear on his website, www.TruthBearer.org) that he has not been subject to the same intense

---

[5] Elise Soukup, "Polygamists, Unite!" *Newsweek,* 20 March 2006.

persecution as those who practice polygamy as a direct result of Joseph Smith's revelation.

National Court Cases

Interestingly enough, there have been multiple cases in the modern courts, including the Supreme Court, that have or may have an impact on the legality of polygamy. Strangely, some of these cases arise out of the legal questions posited by the homosexual movement in the Unites States. Following are several cases on point:

Romer v. Evans

The *Romer* case involves the passage of a voter constitutional amendment to the Colorado State Constitution. It reads:

> Neither the state of Colorado, through any of its branches or departments, nor any of its agencies, political subdivisions, municipalities or school districts, shall enact, adopt or enforce any statute, regulation, ordinance or policy whereby homosexual, lesbian or bisexual orientation, conduct, practices or relationships shall constitute or otherwise be the basis of, or entitle any person or class of persons to have or claim any minority status, quota preferences, protected status or claim of discrimination.

This Section of the Constitution shall be in all respects self-executing.

The amendment passed by public vote on November 3, 1992.

This amendment to the Colorado Constitution came about after Aspen, Denver, and Boulder, Colorado, had passed ordinances banning discrimination in various categories based on sexual orientation. The Colorado courts enjoined enforcement of the Amendment on the grounds that it violated the Equal Protection Clause of the Constitution. The decision was appealed to the Supreme Court of the United States where it was affirmed. The case is not pertinent to the subject of polygamy except with regards to the comments made in the dissenting opinion.

The dissenting argument written by Justice Scalia and joined by Chief Justice Rehnquist and Justice Thomas concluded that the majority of the citizens of Colorado had voted to "preserve its view of sexual morality statewide, against the efforts of a geographically concentrated and politically powerful minority to undermine it." The Court then went on to note that the constitutions of Arizona, Idaho, New Mexico, Oklahoma, and Utah all did the same thing, and that it was forced upon them by the Congress. The "orientation" that had been prohibited to these states was *polygamy*—and it was *forever* prohibited.

In doing this, Congress had singled out the

moral standards of the minority and subjected them to those of the majority. Justice Scalia went on to say that "the Court's disposition today suggests that these provisions [those in the states' constitutions prohibiting polygamy] are unconstitutional, and that polygamy must be permitted in these States on a state-legislated, or perhaps even local-option, basis—*unless, of course, polygamists for some reason have fewer constitutional rights than homosexuals.*"[6]

After reciting the case law that had upheld not only the anti-polygamy laws of the various states enumerated, but also Idaho's anti-polygamy law (previously quoted), the dissent asked: "Has the Court concluded that the perceived social harm of polygamy is a 'legitimate concern of government,' and the perceived social harm of homosexuality is not?" Finally, the dissent concluded that the arguments of the majority and the law that *Romer* promulgated were yet to explain how the Idaho statute was "not an 'impermissible targeting' of polygamists, but (the much more mild) [Colorado amendment] is an 'impermissible targeting' of homosexuals."

The *Romer* dissent is the first chink in *Reynolds'* armor. As the law develops in the homosexual arena, it will be interesting to see if its logical expansion includes polygamy, as the dissent in *Romer* implies.

---

[6] Emphasis added.

Lawrence et al. v. Texas

This case also involved homosexuality, but the fact pertinent to this discussion is that the Supreme Court decided to strike down the Texas law which opposed the individual rights and actions of homosexuals, again deciding that Texas had no right to prohibit the "socially reprehensible act of a minority," even though the majority was in favor of it. The Supreme Court concluded: "the State cannot demean their existence or control their destiny by making their private sexual conduct a crime." Although the court's decision did not encompass polygamy, it did strike down the Texas law that criminalized certain sexual acts. This is the second chink in *Reynolds'* armor.

The emphasis the courts have placed on the civil rights of homosexuals under the Due Process Clause and Equal Protection Clause of the Constitution may eventually impact the practice of polygamy due to the use of the *Lawrence* case in legal actions involving plural marriage. The reason for this is that cases like *Lawrence* attack the efforts of the majority to criminalize behavior that should not be criminal. Because the anti-bigamy/polygamy acts that have been passed since the Morrill Act of 1862 have attacked the LDS Church's belief in polygamy by criminalizing it, the consequences of cases like *Lawrence* are an inevitable decriminalization of polygamy. The government's trend toward decriminalizing religious behavior continued in the following case.

Gonzales, Attorney General, et al. v. O Centro Espirita Beneficente Uniao Dovegetal et al.

Congress enacted the Religious Freedom Restoration Act of 1993 (RFRA) which prohibits the Federal Government from substantially burdening a person's exercise of religion, except when the Government can "demonstrat[e] that application of the burden to the person (1) [furthers] a compelling government interest; and (2) is the least restrictive means of furthering that . . . interest."[7]

In the *Gonzales* case, an Indian church used a drink called *hoasca* when receiving communion. Hoasca is brewed from plants unique to the Amazon Rainforest and contains DMT, a hallucinogen regulated under the Controlled Substances Act. U.S. Customs officials seized the hoasca shipment to the church and threatened prosecution. The Federal District Court granted relief to the church by ruling against the government, stating that the government failed to demonstrate a compelling interest. The Tenth Circuit Court affirmed, stating that the compelling interest of the government must bend "to the person"—the particular claimant whose sincere exercise of religion is being substantially burdened.

In its decision, the Supreme Court stated that in the enactment of the Religious Freedom Act,

---

[7] A "compelling government interest" means that the government's interest is superior to everything else, to the extent that it would supersede the interests of an organization (religious or otherwise) or an individual.

Congress had looked "beyond broadly formulated interests justifying the general applicability of government mandates, scrutinized the asserted harms, and granted specific exemptions to particular religious claimants." It had similarly held such an exception to general government interests in granting the Amish the right to withdraw their students from public schools in favor of their private religious schools.[8]

Gonzales is a third chink in *Reynolds'* armor. By decriminalizing the use of an hallucinogenic drug—something with obvious social consequences when unregulated—during religious practices, the government cleared the way for decriminalizing all religious practices that don't have obvious social consequences.

Unless reversed by a remarkably conservative Supreme Court, the trend toward religious freedom will inevitably continue toward the legalization (or at least the decriminalization) of polygamy. How will the LDS Church react when the way is clear to once again practice the doctrines the Lord taught in Section 132 of *The Doctrine and Covenants?* Will Congress and state legislatures immediately pass laws against polygamy when the Supreme Court decriminalizes or overturns the *Reynolds* case? And will states change the definition of marriage, amending it from "between a man and a woman" to between "a man and *one*

---

[8] *Wisconsin v. Yoder*, 406 US 205 (1972), 213.

woman"? How will society react to an increasing number of practicing polygamists?

The Utah Court Cases

While only time will answer the first two questions above, the courts are already working to answer the third. Five more cases (four in Utah and one in Pennsylvania) that relate to the practice of polygamy could eventually challenge the *Reynolds* case directly—and establish the legal context in which modern polygamy can be practiced.

Bronson v. Swenson

On December 22, 2004, fundamentalists J. Bronson, D. Cook, and G. Lee Cook entered the Salt Lake County Clerk's office and applied for a marriage license. J. Bronson and G. Lee Cook were already married and so declared. J. Bronson wanted a marriage license issued so that he could marry D. Cook, and G. Lee Cook, his legal wife agreed stating that people in Utah had been practicing polygamy for over a hundred years and they wanted to do the same. The Clerk denied the license on the grounds that the state law prohibited issuing a marriage license to anyone that was already married. They filed suit against the Clerk claiming that "the doctrine of plural marriage, i.e., a man having more than one wife, is ordained of God and is to be encouraged and practiced." Citing the *Law-*

rence case noted above, the suit seeks to overturn the 1879 *Reynolds* decision by the U.S. Supreme Court that upheld the ban on polygamy in Utah.

In an article in *The Salt Lake Tribune,* Pamela Manson quoted Utah's Attorney General as saying, "States can regulate marriage, which was not an issue in the Texas case. Any changes in Utah law allowing plural marriage would have to come from the State Legislature. *Lawrence* doesn't apply because it has to do purely with what went on in the bedroom between consenting adults."[9]

While Utah's Attorney General is correct in stating that states have the right to regulate marriage and that the ban on polygamy in Utah is in its Constitution, the Supreme Court may have to deal with the question posed by *Bronson v. Swenson* because of its application of the free exercise clause in cases dealing with homosexuality. (The U.S. District Court dismissed *Bronson v. Swenson.* At the time of this writing, it is on appeal to the U.S. 10th Circuit Court of Appeals.)

State v. Green

On May 18, 2001, fundamentalist Thomas Arthur Green was convicted on four counts of bigamy and one count of failure to pay child support. On June 24, 2002, he was also convicted of child rape of a 13-year-old girl in 1986. She later

---

[9] Pamela Manson, "Utah Trio Challenges State Laws Banning Polygamy," *The Salt Lake Tribune,* 13 January 2004, Section C, pg. 6.

became his legal wife. By then he had five wives. After his conviction, he was sentenced to five years on the first conviction and five years to life on the second. He served a total of six years and was released on parole on August 7, 2007. The Utah Supreme Court upheld both convictions.

Although the *Lawrence* case was raised in the Utah Supreme Court, the Court ruled that it had no application to the *Green* case. The case was not appealed to the federal court, but it is important because it introduces an increasingly common issue with modern polygamy and its social consequences—underage marriage. Polygamy will likely become socially acceptable only when practiced freely between consenting adults.

State v. Holm

Rodney Holm is a member of the Fundamentalist Church of Jesus Christ of Latter Day Saints. He was employed as a police officer in Hildale, Utah, when he was arrested and charged under the Utah Bigamy Act for his participation in a 1998 spiritual marriage to a young woman named Ruth Stubbs. At the time, Holm was legally married to Stubbs's sister. At the time of the "spiritual sealing," Holm was 32 and Ruth Stubbs was 16; however, age was not an issue in the prosecution. Ruth Stubbs bore Holm three children, after which she left the Hildale community and sued for custody of her children.

The State of Utah convicted Holm of bigamy. In his petition, Holm invoked the *Lawrence* case in his defense. Four of the five Utah Supreme Court Justices rejected the application of the *Lawrence* case; however, Justice Christine Durham, after enumerating multiple examples, disagreed with the majority of the Court, stating that the Utah Statute "oversteps lines protecting the free exercise of religion and the privacy of intimate, personal relationships between consenting adults." This is the fourth chink in *Reyonlds'* armor. The case is on appeal to the 10th Circuit Court and may end up in the United States Supreme Court to determine the inherent legality of the current polygamy laws and the precedence of the *Reynolds* case.

As a result of the questions raised in the *Bronson v. Swenson* and *State v. Holm* cases, the U.S. Supreme Court may eventually have the opportunity of reviewing the *Reynolds* case. Further, because of the dissenting argument by Justice Durham in the *Holm* case, the logical application of Justice Scalia's "free exercise" argument that was applied to homosexuality in the *Lawrence* case could also be applied to polygamy.

State of Utah v. Warren Steed Jeffs

Warren Steed Jeffs, prophet of the Fundamentalist Church of Jesus Christ of Latter Day Saints

(FLDS) was arrested outside Las Vegas, Nevada, on August 28, 2006. Jeffs had not been charged with polygamy, but rather with two counts of assisted rape due to the alleged forced marriage of a 14-year-old girl to her first cousin. Additional charges were filed against Jeffs in Arizona. In addition to the Utah and Arizona charges, a federal grand jury returned an indictment which charged Jeffs with flight to avoid prosecution. Prior to his arrest, he was placed on the FBI's ten most wanted list, was the subject of the show, "America's Most Wanted," and had a $100,000 reward posted for his capture. After eluding arrest for months, a simple traffic stop in Nevada led to Jeff's arrest. He was placed in custody and eventually extradited to St. George, Utah, for trial.

Jeffs' trial began September 13, 2007. Only three prosecution witnesses were called: the "14-year-old" wife (now 21 years old) of Allen Steed, her sister, and a midwife rebuttal witness. Additionally, a tape of one of Jeffs' sermons was played to the jury of seven women and five men. Only one defense witness was called, Allen Steed. Final arguments were held September 21, 2007, and the jury found Jeffs guilty of two felony charges.

As of this writing, Allen Steed has been charged with rape, which he admitted to during his testimony when he acknowledged that he had married his then 14-year-old cousin. This is an example of how government authorities are presently prosecuting polygamists. Jeffs admits living in polygamy, but rather than prosecuting him for that crime, the state chose to pursue the "assisted rape of a minor child" charge because of his alleged arrangement of many marriages of this type.

The Pennsylvania Court Case

Since the early days of the LDS Church, society's primary concern with the practice of polygamy has been immorality, reflected in accusations of licentious behavior, forced marriages, and marriages to underage girls. However, a century of legal cases seems to have established the rules by which society will accept a polygamous relationship—a relationship between legally consenting adults. But what of the children born to parents who practice or believe in polygamy? Do parents believing in an alternative marriage style have the right to educate their children concerning their choice?

Shepp v. Shepp

This case, filed April 7, 2003, involves the right of a father in Hallam, Pennsylvania, (who was a declared fundamentalist) to teach his young daughter the principles and doctrines of polygamy, plural marriage, and multiple wives. In the original court decision, it was ordered that the custody arrangements "fashioned by the court for the parties' minor child" (then ten years old) be adjusted. The mother was allowed to raise the child in the Church of Jesus Christ of Latter-day Saints. The father was prohibited from teaching the child his fundamentalist beliefs.

The Court found that the parties were both "converts to the Mormon faith, married in June of 1992 and divorced in February of 2001. Shortly thereafter, [the] Appellant, who considers himself a fundamentalist because of his belief in polygamy, was excommunicated by the Mormon Church."

In upholding the ruling of the lower court, the Pennsylvania Superior Court found the following:

The issue in this matter, stated in the most basic way, is whether a parent, by advocating a religious practice which is prohibited by law, poses a substantial threat to his child. We find that [the father] does, and that no jurisprudence requires this Court to countenance the hazard posed merely because it occurs in the context of proselytism. As Appellee correctly points out, the United States Supreme Court, addressing the issue of polygamy in a series of cases, has held that First Amendment protections do not extend to immoral or criminal acts despite their sanction by religious doctrine.[10]

---

[10] See *Reynolds v. United States*, 98 U.S. 145 (1878).

However, the Pennsylvania Supreme Court reversed this decision and allowed the polygamist parent to teach his religious beliefs to his daughter because he has a constitutional right to express his religious beliefs, even though bigamy is illegal.

The father presented no cases in favor of the free exercise of his religious beliefs; therefore, the Pennsylvania Courts did not consider the *Lawrence* nor the *Romer* cases, but relied on the *Reynolds* case as the basic law.

Although somewhat technical, the discussion of these legal cases is necessary to demonstrate the broad scope of the questions before the Supreme Courts of the various states and the United States. These questions revolve around three clauses in the Constitution: (1) the Free Exercise of Religion clause; (2) the Equal Protection clause; and (3) the Due Process clause. In an article written after the *Green* case, Jonathan Turley, a Professor of Public Interest Law at George Washington Law School, clarified arguments raised in the *Reynolds* case. His article emphasized the three Constitutional questions raised above. While not in favor or support of polygamy, Turley wrote the following:

[I]n its 1878 opinion in *Reynolds vs. United States,* the court refused to recognize polygamy as a legitimate religious practice, dismissing it in racist and anti-Mormon terms as "almost exclusively a feature of the life of Asiatic and African people." In later decisions, the court declared polygamy to be "a blot on our civilization" and compared it to human sacrifice and "a return to barbarism." Most tellingly, the court found that the practice is "contrary to the spirit of Christianity and of the civilization which Christianity has produced in the Western World."

[However,] [c]ontrary to the court's statements, the practice of polygamy is actually one of the common threads between Christians, Jews and Muslims.

Deuteronomy contains a rule for the division of property in polygamist marriages. Old Testament figures such as Abraham, David, Jacob and Solomon were all favored by God and were all polygamists. Solomon truly put the "poly" to polygamy with 700 wives and 300 concubines. Mohammed had 10 wives, though the Koran limits multiple wives to four. Martin Luther at one time accepted polygamy as a practical necessity. Polygamy is still present among Jews in Israel, Yemen and the Mediterranean.

Indeed, studies have found polygamy present in 78% of the world's cultures,

including some Native American tribes.
(While most are polygynists—with one
man and multiple women—there are poly-
andrists in Nepal and Tibet in which one
woman has multiple male spouses.) As
many as 50,000 polygamists live in the
United States.

Given this history and the long religious traditions, it cannot be seriously
denied that polygamy is a legitimate religious belief. Since polygamy is a criminal
offense, polygamists do not seek marriage
licenses. However, even living as married
can send you to prison. Prosecutors have
asked courts to declare a person as married under common law and then convicted them of polygamy.

Declaring a person married under the common law and then convicting them of polygamy or
bigamy is what occurred in the *Green* case.

Concluding his article, Mr. Turley stated, "I
personally detest polygamy. Yet if we yield to our
impulse and single out one hated minority, the
First Amendment becomes little more than hype
and we become little more than hypocrites. For
my part, I would rather have a neighbor with different spouses than a country with different standards for its citizens."[11]

[11] Jonathan Turley, "Polygamy Laws Expose Our Own Hypocrisy," *USA Today*, 3 October 2004.

There is no question that in most instances, the state courts do and will continue to rely on the *Reynolds* case with regard to polygamy until the Supreme Court accepts a case that raises the question of whether the *Reynolds* case will remain the law in our country. There is no doubt that the rulings in the *Lawrence, Romer, Yoder,* and *Gonzales* cases, and the dissenting argument made by Justice Durham in the *Holm* case will impact the Supreme Court when it finally agrees to hear a polygamy case that challenges the *Reynolds* decision.

After all is said and done, it is unlikely that the long-standing, moral tradition in the United States of one wife and one husband will be overturned anytime soon by any court in the land, especially considering the movement in many states and Congress to pass legislation defining marriage as between one woman and one man in an attempt to curb homosexual demands. Some dissenters, like Utah Supreme Court Justice Durham in the *Holm* case, and United States Supreme Court Justice Scalia in the *Romer* case, will continue to speak out as the obvious disparity between polygamists and other minorities continues to widen. It appears obvious, however, that if a proper case involving polygamy comes before the Court, the Court will eventually decriminalize polygamy rather than legalize it.

As a practical matter, polygamists already walk

unmolested in many areas of the country. Anti-polygamy activity that includes hot-button social issues such as marriage to children (statutory rape), as in the *Jeffs* case, tends to sensationalize the polygamy issue and exacerbate the newsworthiness of the situation. You can walk through Costco or Wal-Mart on any given day in St. George, Utah, or other locations in the U.S. and see polygamist men and women shopping. Most people ignore them. Others stare at those polygamists who adhere to what has become known as "fundamentalist fashion" (commonly long braided hair done up on the head with older women and hanging loose on younger girls and basic, longer dresses with full-length sleeves and high necklines on all women). However, many polygamists live and shop in many areas of the United States and Canada, giving no outward indication that they are active participants in polygamist relationships. In appearance, they are indiscernible from any other family in North America.

Interestingly enough, the decriminalization of polygamy would actually lessen its influence on politics. Ideally, anything that cannot be legally discriminated against (gender, race, religious beliefs, sexual orientation, etc.) eventually becomes something that the majority doesn't worry about. Our society certainly isn't perfect, but women vote and enjoy careers; African Americans enjoy education, political office, and social influence;

homosexuals cannot be refused employment and may soon enjoy the legal benefits of marriage; and people of all religions enjoy the privileges of our society. We live in a world where both "polyga-mist" and "polyandrous" relationships (not mar-riages) are popular forms of erotic fantasy—a form of entertainment between consenting adults which the law in some states protects, and both politics and most Americans completely ignore. It appears that the simplest way to remove polygamy as an issue is to legalize it, which may soon be the case in Canada.

Canada

Canada views the polygamy issue much differently than does the Government of the United States. There is a movement in Canada to recognize polygamous marriages as legal, or to at least decriminalize them. As a practical matter, Canada may as well take this action; the Fundamentalist Church of Jesus Christ of Latter-day Saints has been openly practicing polygamy in Bountiful, British Columbia, Canada, for more than sixty years.

In a study commissioned by the Canadian Justice Department, three law professors at Ontario's Queen's University Faculty of Law authored a report urging the Canadian government to legalize polygamy. The paper argued that "the Criminal Code banning polygamy serves no useful purpose and in any case is rarely prosecuted."[12] Their principal reason for such a recommendation was the protection of women and children in these relationships. The study was commissioned after the Canadian government legalized same-sex marriages in 2005.

In an interview with *The Canadian Press*, Martha Bailey, the study's chief author, stated, "Why criminalize the behaviour? . . . We don't criminalize adultery. In light of the fact that we have a fairly permissive society, why are we singling out that particular form of behaviour for criminalization?"[13]

The Bailey report also concluded that the courts might well rule that Canada's law banning polygamy was a violation of its constitutional guarantee of freedom of religion. British Columbia's Attorney General agreed with this conclusion in a *CanWest News Service* report on February 4, 2005. He warned that "Canada's law prohibiting polygamy will not stand up to a legal challenge, because of potential conflicts with laws protecting religious freedoms." He went on to say, "There might well be a case where the court would have to deal with religious freedoms arguments, and I think there is at least some risk that those argu-

---

[12] "Should Canada Decriminalize Polygamy and Plural Unions?" *Polygamy in Canada: Legal and Social Implications for Women and Children—A Collection of Policy Research Reports,* Status of Women Canada (Ottawa, Ontario, Canada).

[13] Dean Beeby, "Study Recommends Repealing Polygamy Ban in Canada," *The Canadian Press,* 12 January 2006.

ments might succeed." Contrary to this opinion, the special prosecutor for the Canadian Attorney General's office recommended that the government "take the polygamy issue straight to court," concluding that many other legal reports believe the law will be upheld.[14]

In addition to the research report, a "Member of Parliament Briefing Note" prepared November 24, 2006, listed fourteen bullet-point key messages identifying the legalization of polygamy argument. All of this followed a publication study by The Vanier Institute of the Family, University of Lethbridge, which concluded that one of five Canadians either approved or accepted polygamist relationships.[15] Even a private group, the "Status of Women Canada's Policy Research Fund" has provided the funding for an extensive study of polygamy in Canada.[16] The Canadians are obviously taking a different approach to the problem of plural marriage and it is equally obvious that Canada will decriminalize and eventually legalize polygamy soon.

As noted earlier, when the U.S. Government persecuted the LDS Church with the anti-polygamy

---

[14] "Canada: Should Polygamists be Tolerated, or Arrested," *The Week*, 31 August 2007, 12.

[15] Study released January 25, 2005, to the Canadian press, available on the Institute's website: www.VIFamily.ca.

[16] Angela Campbel; Nicholas Bala; Katherine Duvall-Antonacopoulos; Leslie MacRae; Joanne J. Paetsch; Martha Bailey; Beverley Baines; Bita Amani; Amy Kaufman. *Polygamy in Canada: Legal and Social Implications for Women and Children: A Collection of Policy Research Reports.* Ottawa: Status of Women Canada, January 2005.

legislation of the nineteenth century, the church approved settlements in Canada, although none of the current Canadian polygamists are members of the LDS Church. It stands to reason that many of the polygamist organizations and churches in existence today would likely relocate to Canada if it decriminalized or legalized the practice of polygamy.

Chapter Eleven _____
Do the Mormons Believe
in Polygamy Today?

Do Mormons still believe in polygamy? Yes. Do they practice polygamy? No! The authorized practice of polygamy definitely ended when the second Manifesto was issued in 1904.

Even though the LDS Church believed the Lord directed the practice to cease when the church was faced with destruction by the U.S. Government, at least four circumstances verify the fact that the church still believes in the doctrine of polygamy as recorded in Section 132 of *The Doctrine and Covenants.*

First: Section 132 of *The Doctrine and Covenants* remains a part of the official scriptures of the LDS Church.

Second: A man may be "sealed" in a temple ceremony to a second woman under the new and everlasting covenant of marriage after the death of his first wife, thereby being married eternally to more than one wife.

Third: A man may be "sealed" to a second living wife after he has been civilly divorced from his first wife without a cancellation of the first sealing, thereby being sealed eternally to two living women at the same time, yet only civilly married to (and cohabiting with) one. To accomplish this, the man must petition the LDS Church's First Presidency to authorize the second temple sealing. In a modern application of the LDS Law of Sarah, the first wife is contacted and her approval sought. If she approves the second sealing, and does not petition for a cancellation of the first sealing, the First Presidency grants the request. If she does not approve of the second sealing, or does not respond to efforts to contact her, the First Presidency will choose whether or not to authorize the second sealing.

Fourth: The LDS Church also performs polygamous marriages (temple sealings) by proxy on behalf of the dead in situations where in life, a man loses his first wife through death or divorce and he remarries. If the second wife is lost to death or divorce, he can marry again, and so forth—yet after they all are dead, he can be sealed to all of the wives.

Let me emphasize again that the LDS Church does not practice nor condone polygamy temporally (while the husband and wives are all alive). As a result of the Manifestos from President Wilford Woodruff and President Joseph F. Smith, the Church of Jesus Christ of Latter-day Saints will excommunicate any member of the church who is actively practicing or preaching polygamy today. Both presidents confirmed that the Manifestos were presented to church members in an LDS General Conference under the direction of the Lord, and both were reported as being unanimously sustained (although there have been some who claim that when the first Manifesto was initially presented, a small minority voted against it and others abstained from voting). It is also true that some members did not like the fact that the church was giving up the practice. The church believes that the practice of polygamy was commanded by God. Multiple quotes by its leading authorities have been presented in this text that prove that fact. No claim has ever been made by the church or its active members that the revelation given to the Prophet Joseph Smith was false, or that the principle should be removed from the church's doctrine.

Because the LDS Church practiced plural marriage for more than fifty years during the nineteenth century, it will never be completely disassociated from it. It is part of the church's heritage. Mormons believe the Lord had a reason to restore the practice to mankind in the 1830s, and while there may be a plethora of hypothetical explanations presented as to why, the only reason that matters to the Mormons is that it was a commandment from God, as the revelation in Section 132 states.

Conclusion _____

This book began by asking if polygamy was a political or a religious issue. From the material presented it is obvious that it is both: religious because Mormons believe the revelation contained in Section 132 of *The Doctrine and Covenants* came from God, and political since both private individuals, state governments, and the federal government have assailed the practice of polygamy almost from its inception.

To faithful members of The Church of Jesus Christ of Latter-day Saints, polygamy is merely one of the many commandments God has given to His Saints in what they believe is the latter days;[1] yet as a church, they believe in honoring and sustaining the laws of the land.[2] This includes the Constitutional right they and others have to challenge laws they feel are unconstitutional. As it states in the church's Eleventh Article of Faith, "We claim the privilege of worshiping Almighty God accord-

_____

[1] Members of the LDS Church call the period from 1820 on the "latter days," or "the dispensation of the fullness of times."

[2] PofGP 1981, Article of Faith 1:12.

ing to the dictates of our own conscience, and allow all men the same privilege, let them worship how, where, or what they may."[3]

We live in a country with a rich history of diversity. Under our Constitution, people are allowed to hold violently opposing beliefs. Consequently, so long as Americans are allowed to govern themselves, there will always be individuals or groups who will harangue prominent members of the church, especially over the issue of polygamy. Like the witches in Shakespear's *McBeth,* they will continue to stir the pot of historical data to see if any of the ingredients rise to the surface and cause a "stink unto heaven" in an attempt to sway people away from anything "Mormon."

Perhaps the nation's fascination with polygamy would abate if it were nothing more than an esoteric doctrine of one church that occasionally appeared on the news, but this will never be the case so long as Mormons continue to believe in the concept, antagonists continue to oppose it, evil men continue to abuse it, and politicians continue to provide a platform for it. Polygamy generates inexorable passions—not only in religious circles but in society in general—and those passions flood over into the political arena whenever Mormonism is involved.

It is easy to be biased on either side of the polygamy issue. Rowenna Erickson, an ex-polyga-

---

[3] PofGP 1981, Article of Faith 1:11.

mist, is quoted as saying, "Polygamy is a big lie, it isn't from God. It never was and it never will be. What kind of a god would create that."[4] In contrast, Mark Henkel of Truthbearer.org champions the "fight for polygamy rights" for Christian conservatives.[5]

When the subject of polygamy is raised, it is hard to remain neutral. The concept generates *sides:* religious sides, social sides, moral sides, and political sides. Mitt Romney is only the latest member of The Church of Jesus Christ of Latter-day Saints to campaign for a major political office, but should he win the Republican nomination in 2008, the Mormon enigma of polygamy will once again rear its controversial head.

---

[4] Pamela Manson, "Utah Trio Challenges State Law Banning Polygamy," *The Salt Lake Tribune,* January 13, 2004, pp C-6.

[5] Mark Henkel, "Important Questions & Media Credibility," Truthbearer.org.

Appendix A _____

Old Testament Polygamists[1]

Abijah

A king of Judah. Fourteen wives. "But Abijah waxed mighty, and married fourteen wives, and begat twenty and two sons, and sixteen daughters." (2 Chronicles 13:21.)

Abraham

"Father of the faithful." Three wives: Sarah, Hagar and Keturah. "Now Sarai Abram's wife bare him no children: and she had an handmaid, an Egyptian, whose name was Hagar." (Genesis 16:1.) "And Sarai Abram's wife took Hagar her maid the Egyptian, after Abram had dwelt ten years in the land of Canaan, and gave her to her husband Abram to be his wife." (Genesis 16:3.) "Then again Abraham took a wife, and her name was Keturah." (Genesis 25:1.) It is possible that Keturah was taken to wife after the death of Sarah; (Genesis 23:1–2) however, Abraham also had multiple concubines. (Genesis 25:6.) The exact number is unknown.

Ahab

Ahab was a king of Israel. In 1 Kings 20:3 it states: "Thy silver and thy gold is mine; thy wives also and thy children, even the goodliest, are mine."

---

[1] Information compiled from the King James version of the Bible.

Ahasuerus

A king of Persia. Possibly also known as King Xerxes. Wives: Vashti, Esther, and various concubines. "Also Vashti the queen made a feast for the women in the royal house which belonged to king Ahasuerus." (Esther 1:9; 2:3, 14, 17.)

Ashur

Two wives. "And Ashur the father of Tekoa had two wives, Helah and Naarah." (1 Chronicles 4:5.)

Belshazzar

A king of Babylon who made a "great feast." He commanded that vessels taken from the temple in Jerusalem be brought forth, ". . . that the king, and his princes, his wives, and his concubines, might drink therein." (Daniel 5:2. Emphasis added.)

Caleb

Caleb had five wives. "And Caleb the son of Hezron begat children of Azubah his wife, and of Jerioth: her sons are these; Jesher, and Shobab, and Ardon. And when Azubah was dead, Caleb took unto him Ephrath, which bare him Hur. (1 Chronicles 2:18–19) . . . And Ephah, Caleb's concubine," (1 Chronicles 2:46) and also "Maachah, Caleb's concubine." 1 Chronicles 2:48.)

David

King David of Israel had at least 18 wives: Michal, Abigail, Ahinoam of Jezreel, Eglah, Maacah, Abital, Haggith, Bathsheba, and ten concubines. "Wherefore David arose and went, he and his men, and slew of the Philistines two hundred men; and David brought their foreskins, and they gave them in full tale to the king, that he might be the king's son in law. And Saul gave him Michal his daughter to wife. (1 Samuel 18:27; see also 1 Samuel 25:44 and 2 Samuel

3:13–14) . . . David sent and communed with Abigail, to take her to him to wife. (1 Samuel 25:42) . . . David also took Ahinoam of Jezreel; and they were also both of them his wives." (1 Samuel 25:43.) His third wife was "Maacah the daughter of Talmai king of Geshur." (2 Samuel 3:3.) His fourth wife was, Haggith; the fifth, Abital; and the sixth, Eglah. (2 Samuel 3:4–5.) "And David took him more concubines and wives out of Jerusalem after he was come from Hebron." (2 Samuel 5:13; 1 Chronicles 14:3.) ". . . And Nathan said to David, Thou art the man. Thus saith the LORD God of Israel, I anointed thee king over Israel, and I delivered thee out of the hand of Saul; And I gave thee thy master's house, and thy master's wives into thy bosom, and gave thee the house of Israel and of Judah; and if that had been too little, I would moreover have given unto thee such and such things." (2 Samuel 12:7–8.) "And David comforted Bathsheba his wife (2 Samuel 12:24) . . . And the king went forth, and all his household after him. And the king left ten women, which were concubines, to keep the house." (2 Samuel 15:16; see also 2 Samuel 16:21–23.) It is interesting to note that Nathan, in condemning David's liaison with Bathsheba and his part in Uriah's death, indicated that the Lord would have given David more possessions than those he already had, including wives and concubines, if he had not sinned.

Elkanah
Two wives: "And he had two wives; the name of the one was Hannah, and the name of the other Peninnah." (1 Samuel 1:2.)

Esau
Six wives: Judith, Adah, Aholibamah, Zibeon, Bashemath and Mahalath. "And Esau was forty years old when he took to wife Judith the daughter of Beeri the Hittite, and Bashemath the daughter of Elon the Hittite: . . ." (Gene-

sis 26:34.) "Then went Esau unto Ishmael, and took unto the wives which he had Mahalath the daughter of Ishmael Abraham's son, the sister of Nebajoth, to be his wife." (Genesis 28:9; 36:1–14.)

Ezra

Two wives. "And the sons of Ezra were, Jether, and Mered, and Epher, and Jalon: and she bare Miriam, and Shammai, and Ishbah the father of Eshtemoa. And his wife Jehudijah bare Jered the father of Gedor, and Heber the father of Socho, and Jekuthiel the father of Zanoah. And these are the sons of Bithiah the daughter of Pharaoh, which Mered took." (1 Chronicles 4:17–18.) It is assumed that because of the separation of the list of sons by inserting a wife's name that the first sons listed were of another wife.

Gideon

A judge of Israel. "And Gideon had threescore and ten sons of his body begotten: for he had many wives." (Judges 8:30.)

Jacob

Jacob's name was changed to Israel by the Lord. He was the father of twelve sons (the twelve tribes of Israel) and had four wives. "And it came to pass in the evening, that he [Leah's father] took Leah his daughter, and brought her to him [Jacob]; and he went in unto her." (Genesis 29:23.) "And Jacob . . . fulfilled her week: and he gave him Rachel his daughter to wife also." (Genesis 29:28.) "And she gave him Bilhah her handmaid to wife: and Jacob went in unto her." (Genesis 30:4.) "When Leah saw that she had left bearing, she took Zilpah her maid, and gave her Jacob to wife." (Genesis 30:9.)

Jehoiachin

A king of Judah. "And he carried away Jehoiachin to Babylon, and the king's mother, and the king's wives, and his officers, and the mighty of the land, those carried he into captivity from Jerusalem to Babylon." (2 Kings 24:15.)

Jehoram
"Behold, with a great plague will the LORD smite thy people, and thy children, and thy wives, and all thy goods." (2 Chronicles 21:14.)

Jerahmeel
Two wives. "Jerahmeel had also another wife, whose name was Atarah; she was the mother of Onam." (1 Chronicles 2:26.)

Joash
Two wives. "And Jehoiada took for him two wives; and he begat sons and daughters." (2 Chronicles 24:3.)

Lamech
Two wives. "And Lamech took unto him two wives: the name of the one was Adah, and the name of the other Zillah." (Genesis 4:19.)

Manasseh
Two wives. "The sons of Manasseh; Ashriel, whom she bare: (but his concubine the Aramitess bare Machir the father of Gilead . . ." (1 Chronicles 7:14.) Again, the language construction would indicate two separate wives.

Mered
Two wives: Bithiah and Hodiah. "[A]nd she bare Miriam, and Shammai, and Ishbah the father of Eshtemoa. And . . . Bithiah the daughter of Pharaoh, which Mered took. And the sons of his wife Hodiah the sister of Naham. . . ." (1 Chronicles 4:17–19.) The language construction again indicates separate wives.

Moses
Two wives. "And Moses was content to dwell with the man: and he gave Moses Zipporah his daughter." (Exodus 2:21; 18:1–6.) "And Miriam and Aaron spake against Moses because of the Ethiopian woman whom he had married: for he had married an Ethiopian woman." (Numbers 12:1.) There is no evidence to indicate whether Zipporah is alive or dead when Moses marries the Ethiopian woman.

Nahor
Two wives. "And it came to pass after these things, that it was told Abraham, saying, Behold, Milcah, she hath also born children unto thy brother Nahor; . . . these eight Milcah did bear to Nahor, Abraham's brother. And his concubine, whose name was Reumah, she bare also Tebah, and Gaham, and Thahash, and Maachah." (Genesis 22: 20–24.)

Rehoboam
Seventy-eight wives. "And Rehoboam took him Mahalath the daughter of Jerimoth . . . and Abihail the daughter of Eliab . . . he took Maachah the daughter of Absalom . . . And Rehoboam loved Maachah the daughter of Absalom above all his wives and his concubines: (for he took eighteen wives, and threescore concubines; and begat twenty and eight sons, and threescore daughters.) . . . And he desired many wives." (2 Chronicles 11:18–23.)

Saul
Two wives. "And the name of Saul's wife was Ahinoam, the daughter of Ahimaaz: and the name of the captain of his host was Abner, the son of Ner, Saul's uncle." (1 Samuel 14:50.) "And Saul had a concubine, whose name was Rizpah, the daughter of Aiah: and Ishbosheth said to Abner, Wherefore hast thou gone in unto my father's concubine?" (2 Samuel 3:7.)

Shaharaim
Two wives. "And Shaharaim begat children in the country of Moab, after he had sent them away; Hushim and Baara were his wives." (1 Chronicles 8:8.)

Simeon
Two wives. "And the sons of Simeon; Jemuel, and Jamin, and Ohad, and Jachin, and Zohar, and Shaul the son of a Canaanitish woman." (Genesis 46:10, Exodus 6:15.) Once again the language construction would indicate separate wives.

Solomon
One thousand wives. "And he had seven hundred wives, princesses, and three hundred concubines: and his wives turned away his heart." (1 Kings 11:3.)

Zedekiah
Multiple wives. "So they shall bring out all thy wives and thy children to the Chaldeans. . . ." (Jeremiah 38:23.)

The following men appear to have multiple wives by implication:

Eliphaz
Two wives. "And . . . Timna was concubine to Eliphaz, Esau's son. . . . " It would be logical to assume that he had a wife as well as a concubine. (Genesis 36:11–12.)

Heman
By implication from the number of his sons and daughters. "And God gave to Heman fourteen sons and three daughters." (1 Chronicles 25:5.)

Hosea
"So he went and took Gomer the daughter of Diblaim; which

conceived, and bare him a son." (Hosea 1:3.) "Then said the LORD unto me, Go yet, love a woman beloved of her friend, yet an adulteress, according to the love of the LORD toward the children of Israel, who look to other gods, and love flagons of wine." (Hosea 3:1.) Some might interpret the second unnamed wife as a symbolic rendering of the condition of Israel at the time.

Ibzan
By implication from the number of his sons and daughters. "And he had thirty sons, and thirty daughters, whom he sent abroad, and took in thirty daughters from abroad for his sons. And he judged Israel seven years." (Judges 12:9.)

Jair
By implication from the number of his sons. "And he had thirty sons that rode on thirty ass colts, and they had thirty cities, which are called Havothjair unto this day, which are in the land of Gilead." (Judges 10:4.)

Shimei
By implication from the number of children. "And Shimei had sixteen sons and six daughters; but his brethren had not many children, neither did all their family multiply, like to the children of Judah." (1 Chronicles 4:27.)

Ziba
By inference due to the number of his sons. "Now Ziba had fifteen sons and twenty servants." (2 Samuel 9:10.)

Appendix B_____
Joseph Smith's Wives

Marital Status
This term refers to a woman's civil status at the time she married Joseph Smith. If her status is "married," it means she was married civilly to another man at the time she was married to Smith. A marriage for "time" or "time only" ends with the death of either spouse. A marriage for "eternity" lasts forever.

Polygamy
Meaning: "many marriages." A man is married to more than one woman at the same time. Another term the Mormons used for this type of union was "plural marriage." Anthropologically, polygamy is divided into two subcategories: polygyny and polyandry.

Polygyny
Meaning: "many women." A man is married to two or more women at the same time.

Polyandry
Meaning: "many men." In the condition called "polyandry," a woman is married to multiple husbands at the same time

Proxy
When a living person is sealed for eternity to, or on behalf

of, a deceased person, or the living surrogate in a proxy sealing.

Well-Documented Wives
Information in this Appendix is presented in the following order: wife's name (names of husbands in order), *marriage date, status at the time of marriage, age at the time of marriage, extant husband (if any)*, and notes. Only well-documented wives are listed.

1. Emma Hale (Smith-Bidamon): *January 1827, single, 22.* Joseph Smith's first wife with whom he had eight children. Only a few survived to adulthood. After Joseph's death, Emma married Lewis Crum Bidamon, not a member of the LDS Church.

2. Fanny Alger (Smith-Custer): *early 1833, single, 16.* Fanny separated from Joseph Smith and married Solomon Custer, a non-member of the LDS Church. Fanny and Solomon had nine children. No children are known to Fanny and Joseph.

3. Lucinda Pendleton (Morgan-Harris-Smith): *about 1838, married, age approximately 37, George Harris.* Lucinda was married to George Washington Harris after the murder of her first husband, Capt. William Morgan. She remained with polyandrous first husband George Harris (LDS Church member), but was married by proxy in the Nauvoo Temple to Joseph Smith. She later divorced Harris.

4. Louisa Beaman (Smith-Young): *5 April 1841, single, 26.* Louisa was in disguise (a man's hat and coat) at her wedding ceremony. After Joseph's death, she married Brigham Young. She had five children by Brigham, all of whom preceded her in death. She died of breast cancer at age 35.

5. Zina Diantha Huntington (Jacobs-Smith-Young): *27 October 1841, married, 20, Henry Jacobs.* Zina was sealed to Joseph Smith while seven months pregnant with the child of her first husband, Henry Bailey Jacobs. She remained with her polyandrous first husband until the death of the prophet. She left Jacobs in 1846 to marry Brigham Young. Jacobs witnessed her sealings to Brigham Young for "time" and to Joseph Smith "for eternity" in the Nauvoo Temple.

6. Prescendia Lathrop Huntington (Buell-Smith-Kimball): *11 December 1841, married, 31, Normal Buell.* Prescendia married Norman Buell in 1828. They had several children. They converted to Mormonism around 1836. He eventually apostatized from the church. She had a polyandrous proxy marriage to Joseph Smith in 1841, but stayed with Buell for nineteen years. She eventually left Buell and married Heber C. Kimball on 7 November 1846, with whom she had two children.

7. Agnes Moulton Coolbrith (D. Smith-J. Smith-G. Smith-Pickett): *6 January 1842, widow, 33.* Agnes married Don Carlos Smith, Joseph's youngest brother, in 1835. They had three daughters. She was married to Joseph Smith in 1842. After his death she married his cousin, George A. Smith for time but when he left for Utah, she stayed in Nauvoo. She then married William Pickett in 1847 with whom she had twins. They moved to California where she spent the rest of her life. Pickett was an alcoholic and left her in 1870.

8. Sylvia Sessions (Lyon-Smith-Kimball-Clark): *8 February 1842, married, 23, Windsor Lyon.* Sylvia married Windsor Lyon in 1838. She married Joseph Smith polyandrously in 1842 and bore him one child, Josephine Lyon (Fisher), in 1844. She stayed with Lyon for eleven years, bearing him four children (all of whom died as infants). Sylvia married

Heber C. Kimball for time, polyandrously, on 26 January 1846, but did not go west with him, staying with Lyon. After Lyon's death in 1849, she married non-LDS Ezekiel Clark in 1850. She bore him three children, but left him and moved to Bountiful, Utah, in 1854.

9. Mary Elizabeth Rollins (Lightner-Smith-Young): *late February 1842, married, 23, Adam Lightner.* Mary was a polyandrous wife of Joseph Smith, marrying both Smith and Brigham Young while still cohabiting with her first husband, Adam Lightner. She never left Lightner, even though he was not a Mormon.

10. Patty Bartlett (Sessions-Smith): *9 March 1842, married, 47, David Sessons.* Patty married David Sessions on June 28, 1812. They lived in Maine where he became quite wealthy. Patty had seven children, only three of which lived to become adults. As a trained midwife, she delivered approximately 4,000 babies. When the Sessions moved to Nauvoo, Patty was sealed to Joseph Smith on March 9, 1842, for time and all eternity. Her daughter Sylvia, had married Joseph a month earlier. Patty continued to live with David. They eventually migrated to Utah with the other saints.

11. Marinda Nancy Johnson (Hyde-Smith): *April 1842, married, 27, Orson Hyde.* Marinda married Orson Hyde in 1834 in Kirtland, Ohio. She was married eternally to him in the Nauvoo temple. Later she was sealed eternally by proxy marriage to Joseph Smith. She eventually divorced Hyde.

12. Elizabeth Davis (Goldsmith-Brackenbury-Durfee-Smith-Lott): *About June 1842, married, approximately 50–51, Jabez Durfee.* Elizabeth married her first husband, Gilbert Goldsmith, in 1811. He died the same year leaving her with one son. She then married Joseph Brackenbury between 1815 and 1819. They converted to Mormonism and had five sons. He died in 1831. She married Jabez Durfee in Missouri in 1834 and stayed with him approximately ten years. She married Joseph in 1842 and after his death in 1846, she married Cornelius P. Lott for time and Joseph for eternity by proxy. Her marriage to Lott was short-lived.

13. Sarah Maryetta Kingsley (Howe-Cleveland-Smith): *Earlier than 29 June 1842, married, 53–54 (unverified), John Cleveland.* Sarah married John Howe in 1804 and had one son. John died between 1823 and 1826. She then married John Cleveland in 1826, had two children, and stayed with him the rest of her life. The Nauvoo Temple Record states Sarah was sealed to Joseph Smith for eternity and to John Smith for time in January of 1846.

14. Delcena Johnson (Sherman-Smith-Babbitt): *earlier than July 1842, widowed, 37–38 (unverified).* Delcena married Joseph Smith before July 1842. She was the widow of Lyman Sherman. She bore Lyman six children between 1829 and 1839. After Joseph's death, she married Almon Babbitt, her brother-in-law, for time. She was severely crippled by rheumatoid arthritis, but was able to see Utah just before she died.

15. Eliza Roxey Snow (Smith-Young): *29 June 1842, single, 38. Eliza married Joseph Smith on June 29, 1842.* After Joseph's death, in 1846, Eliza was sealed to Brigham Young in the Nauvoo Temple. She bore him no children. She was a gifted poet and eventually became one of the leading women in the west. She died in 1887.

16. Sarah Ann Whitney (Smith-Kingsbury-Kimball): *27 July 1842, single, 17.* Sarah married Joseph in 1842. He solemnized her marriage to Joseph Kingsbury in 1843, making him technically her polyandrous husband. Although legal, it was a marriage in name only. She later left Kingsbury and was sealed in 1846 to Joseph for eternity and Heber C. Kimball for time only. After Joseph's death, she bore Kimball seven children.

17. Martha McBride (Knight-Smith-Kimball): *August 1842, widowed, 37.* Martha was the widow of Vinson Knight. She had lived with him from 1826 to 1842 and bore him seven children. She was sealed to Joseph Smith in 1842. After his death, she married Heber C. Kimball for time. They had one child that died at birth.

18. Ruth Daggett Vose (Sayers-Smith): *February 1843, married, 33, Edward Sayers.* Ruth married Edward Sayers in 1841 and stay with him until he died in 1861. He was never baptized, but lived with her in Nauvoo, Illinois, and Salt Lake City, Utah. She had no children. She was married to Smith in 1843 polyandrously.

19. Flora Ann Woodworth (Smith-Grove): *Spring 1843, single, 16.* Flora married Joseph in 1843. After his death she married Mr. Grove who was not a member of the church. Flora and Mr. Grove had two or three children.

20. Emily Dow Partridge (Smith-Young): *4 March 1843, single, 19.* Emily married Joseph on March 4, 1843. After his death she married Brigham Young for time and bore him seven children. She was the mother of Don Carlos Young, an architect for the Salt Lake Temple.

21. Eliza Maria Partridge (Smith-Lyman): *8 March 1843, single, 22.* Eliza married Joseph in 1843. After his martyrdom, she married Amasa Lyman and bore him five children. Two of her sisters also married Lyman, but all three sisters left him when he was excommunicated. In later life, she lived in Fillmore and Oak City, Utah.

22. Almera Woodard Johnson (Smith-Barton): *April 1843, single, 30.* Almera married Joseph in 1843. After his death she married Reuben Barton and had five daughters. She left him in 1861 and moved to Utah when he became disaffected with the church. Most of her children died in their youth. None of them married. The one daughter who lived was mentally challenged and lived with Almera for approximately 30 years in Parowan, Utah.

23. Lucy Walker (Smith-Kimball): *1 May 1843, single, 17.* Lucy married Joseph in 1843. After he died, she married Heber C. Kimball for time. They moved to Utah and she bore him nine children.

24. Sarah Lawrence (Smith-Kimball-Mount): *May 1843, single, 17.* Sarah married Joseph in 1843. After his death she married Heber C. Kimball for time, but divorced him in 1851 in Utah. She then married Joseph Mount in 1853 and moved to Napa, California, where she left the church. She had no children by any of her husbands.

25. Maria Lawrence (Smith-Young-Babbitt): *May 1843, single, 19.* Maria married Joseph Smith in 1843. When he died, she married Brigham Young (according to some sources), then married Almon Babbitt in 1846. She had no children.

26. Helen Mar Kimball (Smith-Whitney): *May 1843, single, 14.* Helen married Joseph in 1843. After he died, she married Horace Whitney in 1846 for time. She bore him eleven children, among them Apostle Orson E. Whitney. She loathed polygamy as a young teenager in Nauvoo, but as an older woman in Utah, she wrote two pamphlets in its defense.

27. Hannah Ells (Smith): *1843, single, 29–30.* Hannah never remarried after Joseph's death.

28. Elvira Annie Cowles (Holmes-Smith): *1 June 1843, married, 29, Jonathan Holmes.* Elvira remained with her first husband, Jonathan Holmes, a member of the church, until her death. Most of her later life was lived in Farmington, Utah. She married Joseph Smith polyandrously in 1843.

29. Rhoda Richards (Smith-Young): *12 June 1843, single, 58.* Rhoda married Joseph in 1843. When he died, she was married to Brigham Young for time, but never cohabited with him. She lived with relatives in Salt Lake City, Utah, for the rest of her life.

30. Desdemona Catlin Wadsworth Fullmer (Smith-Benson-McLane): *July 1843, single, 32–33.* Desdemona married Joseph Smith in 1843. After he was martyred, she married Ezra Taft Benson for time in 1846. The marriage did not last. She then married Harrison Parker McLane in 1852 and bore him a son. This marriage also ended in separation. She died in Salt Lake City, Utah.

31. Olive Grey Frost (Smith-Young): *summer 1843, single, perhaps 27–28.* Olive married Joseph Smith in 1843. She was one of the early female missionaries in Mormon history. She married Brigham Young for time on November 7, 1844, but died of malaria less than a year later.

32. Melissa Lott (Smith-Bernhisel-Willis): *20 September 1843, single, 19.* Melissa married Joseph in 1843. After he died, she married John Bernhisel, a prominent LDS politician, but the marriage did not last. She later married Ira Willis in 1849 and settled in Lehi, Utah. They had seven children. Ira and one of their sons died in a farming accident in 1863.

33. Nancy Maria Winchester (Smith-Kimball-Arnold): *perhaps 1842 or 1843, single, may have been 14.* Nancy married Joseph Smith, but the exact date is unknown. After he died, she married Heber C. Kimball for time in 1844 (when she was sixteen). The marriage did not produce children, so Heber helped arrange her marriage to Amos George Arnold in 1865. They had one child.

34. Fanny Young (Carr-Murray-Smith): *2 November 1843, widowed, 56.* Fanny was the older sister of Brigham Young. She married Joseph in 1843 and was his last known plural wife. She had married Robert Carr in 1803 and was either widowed or divorced by 1827. She then married Rossell Murray in 1832. After his death in 1839 or 1840, she married Joseph. She moved to Utah and lived in the Lion House, one of Brigham Young's homes, until her death.

Many of the marriages of the above thirty-four documented wives to Joseph Smith were sealings, not connubial marriages. The records are not always clear as to which were cohabiting with the prophet and which were only sealed to him, but it appears that marriages 3, 5, 6, 8, 9, 10, 18, 28 were only sealings (technically polyandrous but the wife remained with her first husband).

Sources: the terms and list of well-documented wives Nos. 2–34 were adapted from Todd Compton in his book, *In Sacred Loneliness: The Plural Wives of Joseph Smith* [Salt Lake City: Signature Books, 1997], 4–9 with some additions and deletions (used with permission).

Additional information taken from Fawn M. Brodie, *No Man Knows My History* (New York: Alfred A. Knopf, 1945) and Newell C. Bringhurst, *Reconsidering No Man Knows My History, Fawn M. Brodie and Joseph Smith in Retrospect* (Logan: Utah State University Press, August 1996).

Appendix C _____
A Chronology of Modern Polygamy

1835   The Article on Marriage is published. Among oth-
       er information, it states, ". . . we believe that one
       man should have one wife, and one woman but one
       husband, except in case of death, when either is at
       liberty to marry again." (HC 2:247.)

1843   The revelation on celestial marriage contained in
       Section 132 of *The Doctrine and Covenants* is re-
       corded by Joseph Smith.

1846   A large contingent of Mormons are in Winter Quar-
       ters on the banks of the Missouri River. They are
       in the process of being driven out of Nauvoo, Illi-
       nois, and migrating to the Great Salt Lake Valley.
       Although some are living in polygamy, it has not
       been publicly acknowledged.

1849   The petition for the State of Deseret is rejected by
       Congress.

1850   A geographically smaller Territory of Utah is ap-
       proved with Brigham Young as the Territorial Gov-
       ernor. Young is known to have multiple wives.

1852   Brigham Young publicly reveals the revelation on
       celestial marriage (Section 132 of *The Doctrine and*

Covenants) in a General Conference of the LDS Church held on August 29, 1852. Orson Pratt, an LDS apostle, delivers a public discourse wherein he describes the doctrine as "one of the best doctrines ever proclaimed to any people." (JD 1:53.)

1853   Orson Pratt publishes *The Seer* in Washington D.C., which contains Joseph Smith's revelation on plural marriage. (Orson Pratt, *The Seer,* January 1852.)

1856   The abolishment of the "Twin Relics of Barbarism, Slavery and Polygamy," is selected as the Republican party's national platform. (Orma Lindord, "The Mormons and the Law: The Polygamy Cases," *Utah Law Review,* 312.)

The second proposal for Utah's statehood is rejected.

1862   The third State of Deseret constitution is written as a bid for statehood. The bid is rejected by Congress, but the State of Deseret continues for eight years after the territorial legislature adjourns.

The first federal law outlawing polygamy, the Morrill Anti-Bigamy Law, is signed by Abraham Lincoln on July 8, 1862.

1866   The Wade bill contains provisions to diminish the power of local government, but it does not pass Congress.

1868   The proposed Cragin bill includes many features of the Wade bill. It also includes a provision to abolish trial by jury in all cases under the Morrill Anti-Bigamy Act. The bill is withdrawn in favor of the Cullom bill.

1869   The Cullom bill incorporates most of the provision of the Cragin bill, but declares cohabitation a misdemeanor and includes provisions to deprive plural wives of immunity as witnesses in cases involving their husbands. It also allows the president to send U.S. Army troops into Utah and raise a 25,000 man militia in the territory to enforce the law. The bill does not pass.

The transcontinental railroad is completed at Promontory, Utah, making Utah less isolated.

1870   Women in Utah are given the right to vote.

1874   The Polland Act nullifies all earlier Supreme Court decisions favorable to the Mormons, creates a new jury selection process primarily aimed at limiting Mormon control over the selection of jurors, strips the territorial attorney and territorial marshal of most of their powers, and restricts the jurisdiction of the probate courts in the Territory of Utah.

George Reynolds, Brigham Young's secretary, volunteers to be the defendant in a test case to determine the constitutionality of the Morrill Anti-Bigamy Law.

1875   A contingent of more than twenty-two thousand Utah women petition congress to repeal the Morrill Anti-Bigamy Law.

1877   Brigham Young dies in Salt Lake City, Utah.

1878   Joseph F. Smith states, "I understand the law of celestial marriage to mean that every man in this Church, who has the ability to obey and practice it in righteousness and will not, shall be damned, I say I understand it to mean this and nothing less, and I testify in the name of Jesus that it does mean that." (JD 1967, 20:31.)

1879   Reynolds loses his case testing the constitutionality of the Morrill Anti-Bigamy Law and goes to prison for two years. The Morrill Act of 1862 is declared valid.

1882   The Edmunds Act is passed. It contains the following provisions: polygamy replaces bigamy as a criminal offense; men who simultaneously marry two or more women will be convicted of polygamy; cohabitation becomes a misdemeanor; polygamy and cohabitation can be charged in the same indictment; jurors are disqualified for having or believing in multiple wives; Utah registration and election offices held by Mormons are vacated and provision made for their replacement; polygamists and those involved in cohabitation are denied the right to vote or hold elective or appointed public office; a Utah Commission is created to oversee future elections and issue certificates to those lawfully elected.

1885   Some polygamists move to Mexico and Canada to avoid prosecution.

Idaho's Test Oath Law practically disfranchises all Mormons because of their membership in the LDS Church. It is sustained by the supreme court of the territory four years later. Some LDS Church leaders go into hiding to avoid prosecution.

1886   In a disputed revelation, John W. Woolley claims Joseph Smith and Jesus Christ appeared to John

Taylor extending the keys to sanction plural marriage to the select group of men then meeting in the home of John W. Woolley (rather than being held exclusively by the president of the LDS Church). Many fundamentalist groups claim this revelation as the basis of their authority to practice polygamy. John W. Woolley became known as the "father of Mormon Fundamentalism."

1887   The Edmunds-Tucker Act is passed with the following provisions: a wife can testify against her husband in actions against bigamy, polygamy, or unlawful cohabitation, with some limited exceptions; witnesses can be compelled to appear without a subpoena; prosecution for adultery can be instituted the same way prosecution for other crimes is instituted; every marriage is required to be certified; limitations of jurisdiction on the probate courts are continued; probate judges become presidential appointments; illegitimate children born one year after the passage of the Act cannot inherit; the dower right of the wife to inherit one-third of her deceased husband's assets is reinstated; women are disenfranchised; secret ballots are allowed; the powers of the Utah Commission are reaffirmed; a voter oath in support of the anti-polygamy laws is instituted; control of public education is placed in the hands of federal officials; the Nauvoo Legion is abolished; the LDS Church is disincorporated; the Perpetual Emigrating Fund Company is dissolved and the territorial legislature is prohibited from enacting any law that would bring people into the territory for any purpose.

LDS President John Taylor dies in hiding in Kaysville, Utah.

1890   The Edmunds-Tucker Bill is sustained by the United States Supreme Court, threatening total disfranchisement of the church. This means the church will be dissolved and its property escheated.

President Wilford Woodruff issues the 1890 Manifesto discontinuing the practice of polygamy. Some members of the LDS Church still persisted in living with plural wives. "Hunting cohabs" becomes lucrative employment for those paid to find offenders.

More polygamist families moved to Canada where a community named "Bountiful" is eventually established.

1896   Utah becomes a state.

1898   B.H. Roberts is elected to the House of Representatives for the 56th Congress. His qualifications are challenged since he is a polygamist and a Mormon. He is denied his seat. As a result, Utah has no representation in the 56th Congress.

1903   Reed Smoot is elected as a U.S. Senator. He is not a polygamist. His qualifications are challenged, but he is provisionally seated during his trial. Due to powerful Republican influence, the negative decision of a committee of nine Republicans and five Democrats is overturned and he is allowed to take his seat.

1904   LDS President Joseph F. Smith issues a second "Manifesto" stating that any person solemnizing or entering into plural marriage "will be deemed in transgression against the Church and will be . . . excommunicated therefrom."

1912   Lorin C. Woolley, son of John W. Woolley, gives the first written account of the disputed 1886 visitation by Joseph Smith and Jesus Christ to the then LDS Church President, John Taylor. Woolley later maintains that plural marriage must and will continue.

1913   Short Creek (later called Colorado City, Arizona) is settled by a cattle rancher named Jacob Lauritzen. By 1930 polygamists are firmly settled in the desolate area.

1914   John W. Woolley is excommunicated from the LDS Church for non compliance with the 1890 Manifesto.

1918   John W. Woolley serves as leader of the Fundamentalists until 1928.

1924   Lorin C. Woolley is excommunicated for publicizing that LDS Church leaders took multiple wives after the 1890 Manifesto.

       Polygamist Alma Dayer LeBaron moves his family to northern Mexico to escape U.S. law enforcement. A farm called "Colonia LeBaron is established in Galeana, Chihuahua.

1928   John W. Woolley dies and is succeeded by Lorin C. Wooley as leader of the Fundamentalists.

1934   Lorin C. Woolley dies and is succeeded by J. Leslie Broadbent.

1935   The Lee's Ferry polygamists settle in Short Creek after being excommunicated by the LDS Church for refusing to renounce polygamy. J. Leslie Broadbent dies and is succeeded by John Y. Barlow. He begins the polygamist colony at Short Creek on the Arizona-Utah border. He establishes a United Order where members of the clan share resources. Some disagree with Barlow's appointment resulting in Charles W. Kingston and Eldon Kingston creating a splinter group called the Latter Day Church of Christ, or the "Kingston clan."

An unsuccessful raid by the law fails to stamp out the Fundamentalist colony in Short Creek.

1942   Pursuant to a Declaration of Trust signed by John Y. Barlow, Leroy S. Johnson, J. Marion Hammon, J.W. Musser, and Rulon T. Jeffs, the United Effort Plan Trust is formed by the Fundamentalists. It comprises and manages real property and improvements situated in Colorado City, Arizona; Hildale, Utah; and Bountiful, British Columbia.

1943   The FBI raids Short Creek and fifteen men are sent to the Sugar House penitentiary in Salt Lake City, Utah. Nine win a release by renouncing polygamy. Most return to Short Creek and immediately break their promise. Joseph W. Musser is among them.

1949   John Y. Barlow dies and is succeeded by Joseph W. Musser. Musser leads the polygamous community in and around Salt Lake City, Utah, (this group is later called the Apostolic United Brethren) and Legrand Woolley leads the fundamentalist community at Short Creek (this group becomes the Fundamentalist Church of Jesus Christ of Latter Day Saints under the direction of Leroy S. Johnson). Later, a paralytic stroke partially disables Musser and he designates Rulon C. Allred as his successor. This action predicates a schism in the sect. Ultimately, Musser's successor is Charles Zitting.

1950s   The Canadian polygamists and the Fundamentalists in Colorado City, Arizona, and Hildale, Utah, exchange young women as wives to strengthen ties between the two groups.

1951   Alma Dayer LeBaron dies. He is succeeded by his son, Joel LeBaron, who eventually incorporates the Church of the Firstborn in the Fullness of Times in Salt Lake City, Utah. His younger brother is Ervil LeBaron. The group eventually numbers approximately 30 families in both Utah and a community named Los Molinos on the Baja California Peninsula.

1953   Arizona Governor Howard Pyle orders a massive police raid on Short Creek on July 26, 1953. Newsreels portraying children being separated from their parents results in negative publicity for Pyle, ultimately ending his political career. Twenty-three polygamist men are given only one year of probation. The negative publicity ironically helps Short Creek avoid interference from the law for many years.

1954   Musser dies and Charles Zitting becomes the presiding elder of the FLDS Church. Four months later Zitting dies and Leroy S. Johnson leads the Fundamentalist Church of Jesus Christ of Latter Day Saints. The polygamous community splits into three groups when Musser dies: the FLDS Church which stays in Short Creek; the Apostolic United Brethren which relocates to Bluffdale, Utah, under the direction of Rulon C. Allred; and the United

Latter-day Church which relocates to Lexington, Nebraska, and later to Layton, Utah.

1961   Rulon C. Allred purchases 640 acres of ranch land in the Bitterroot Mountains of Montana with the intent of establishing a united order for the Apostolic United Brethren Church (the Allred Group).

1963   Hildale, Utah, is officially incorporated.

1963   Short Creek officially changes its name to Colorado City, Arizona.

1972   Ervil LeBaron splits from his brother Joel and establishes the Church of the Lamb of God in San Diego, California. He orders his brother Joel killed. Leadership of the Baja group passes to Ervil's younger brother, Verlan, whom Ervil unsuccessfully attempts to have killed over the next ten years.

1975   Ervil LeBaron orders the death of polygamist Bob Simons. LeBaron and one of his wives, Vonda White, are responsible for many ensuing murders, perhaps even his own daughter, Rebecca.

1977   Rulon C. Allred, leader of the Apostolic United Brethren church, is murdered on the orders of Ervil LeBaron, the head of a rival polygamous sect.

1979   Ervil LeBaron is apprehended by police in Mexico and extradited to the United States where is he convicted of Rulon C. Allred's death.

1980   Ervil LeBaron is sentenced to life in prison for Allred's death. While in prison, he continues to order the murder of his opponents, including some of his wives and children. Approximately 25 people are killed as a result of his machinations.

1981   Ervil LeBaron dies in his prison cell. His younger brother Verlan dies in an automobile accident in Mexico City two days after Ervil's body is discovered. Ervil's daughter, Jacqueline Tarsa LeBaron, is currently wanted by the FBI.

1983   The Allred Group (Apostolic United Brethren) incorporates Pinesdale, Montana, close to Hamilton and Missoula. By 1998 they boast more than 800 persons and 250 families.

1984   Leroy S. Johnson dismisses Marion Hammon and Alma Timpson from the Fundamentalist's Priesthood Council. They take many of Johnsons followers with them and eventually establish the town of Centennial Park City, Utah.

1985   Colorado City, Arizona, incorporates.

1986   Leroy S. Johnson dies. He is succeeded by Rulon T. Jeffs. Jeffs, an accountant, eventually sits on the boards of multimillion-dollar corporations, purchases a huge estate in one of Utah's most expensive neighborhoods, fathers more than 60 children, and serves as prophet of the largest polygamist church (FLDS) in North America.

1988   Marion Hammon dies. His successor as leader of the polygamists in Centennial, Utah, is Alma Del Timpson. Timpson calls his son, John Timpson, and Frank Naylor as apostles and Ivan Neilsen as a bishop.

1990   Naylor and Nielsen and their families leave Centennial Park and move to the Salt Lake Valley where they form their own group, with Naylor as their leader.

1994   Birth of the Christian polygamy movement known as Truthbearer.org. The organization has no connection to the LDS Church.

1998   Alma Timpson dies. His son John succeeds him as the leader in Centennial Park.

2000   Tapestry Against Polygamy is organized. This is "a non-profit organization located in Salt Lake City, Utah, that advocates against the human right[s] violations inherent in polygamy and provides assistance to individuals leaving polygamous cults." (Mission Statement on Tapestry Against Polygamy website, www.Polygamy.org.)

2002   Rulon T. Jeffs, FLDS leader, dies in St. George, Utah, of natural causes. His son, Warren Jeffs, proclaims himself prophet and leader of the FLDS Church. Winston Blackmore is dismissed by Jeffs as bishop of the Canada branch of the FLDS Church.

2003   Rodney Holm, a member of the FLDS Church, is convicted of unlawful sexual conduct with a 16- or 17-year-old girl and of one count of bigamy. This is the first legal action against a member of the FLDS Church since the Short Creek raid in 1953.

The FLDS Church purchases "a hunting retreat" four miles northeast of Eldorado, Texas, where they eventually build a temple.

Utah passes a child bigamy bill (HB307). (Child

bigamy is marrying a second wife who is less than 18 years-of-age. It is punishable by 1–15 years in prison.)

2004   Dan Barlow, the mayor of Colorado City, and approximately 20 other men are excommunicated from the FLDS Church and stripped of their wives and children.

A child bigamy statute is adopted by the state of Arizona.

2005   Brent Jeffs files suit accusing Warren Jeffs and two other uncles of sexually assaulting him when he was a child.

Six "lost boys" are cast out of their homes on the Utah-Arizona border to reduce competition for wives. They file suit against the FLDS Church.

The "Status of Women in Canada" study recommends legalizing or decriminalizing polygamy.

British Colombia's Attorney General states that Canada's law criminalizing polygamy won't "stand up" in court tests.

2006   Centennial Park Action Committee is formed in Centennial Part, Arizona, with the goal of decriminalizing polygamy.

Canadian Parliament Briefing Note lists 14 points in favor of legalizing polygamy.

Warren Jeffs is named to the FBI's Ten Most Wanted Fugitives list on charges of sexual misconduct with minors. He is captured on August 28, 2006 on Interstate 15 just north of Las Vegas, Nevada.

2007   Warren Jeffs remains the leader of the FLDS Church, although he is in the custody of the state of Utah after being convicted of being an accomplice to rape. He appeals his case.

Polygamist Allen Steed is charged with first degree rape, a felony.

Bibliography_____

Arrington, Leonard J., and Davis Bitton, *The Mormon Experience: A History of the Latter-day Saints.* New York: Alfred A. Knoph, 1979.

Arizona Constitution, Article XX, Paragraph 2.

Bachman, Daniel W. "A Study of the Mormon Practice of Plural Marriage before the Death of Joseph Smith." Unpublished M.A. thesis. Purdue University, 1975.

Beeby, Dean. "Study Recommend Repealing Polygamy Ban in Canada." *The Canadian Press,* 12 January 2006.

Brodie, Fawn M. *No Man Knows My History.* New York: Alfred A. Knopf, 1945.

Bringhurst, Newell C. *Reconsidering No Man Knows My History, Fawn M. Brodie and Joseph Smith in Retrospect.* Logan: Utah State University Press, August 1996.

Bruce, Alexander Balmain. *A Systematic and Critical Study of the Parables of Our Lord,* 7th ed. London: Hodder and Stoughton, 1897.

By Authority of Congress: the Statutes at Large of the United States of America. Boston: Little, Brown, 1879.

Campbell, Angela; Nicholas Bala; Katherine Duvall-Antonacopoulos; Leslie MacRae; Joanne J. Paetsch; Martha Bailey; Beverley Baines; Bita Amani; Amy Kaufman. *Polygamy in Canada: Legal and Social Implications for Women and Children: A Collection of Policy Research Reports.* Ottawa: Status of Women Canada, January 2005.

Campbell, Eugene E. *Establishing Zion: The Mormon Church in the American West, 1847–1869.* Salt Lake City: Signature Books, 1988.

"Canada: Should Polygamists be Tolerated—or Arrested." *The Week,* 31 August 2007: 12.

Cannon, George Q. Ed. *Juvenile Instructor.* Vol. 34:354.

Church Historical Department. *Historical Record.* Salt Lake City: The Church of Jesus Christ of Latter-day Saints, 1886. Vol. 5:144.

Compton, Todd. *In Sacred Loneliness: The Plural Wives of Joseph Smith.* Salt Lake City: Signature Books, 1997.

Conference Reports. Salt Lake City: The Church of Jesus Christ of Latter-day Saints, 6 April 1904: 74–75.

Congressional Globe. (1860): Appendix: 194, 1492, 1496.

Congressional Record. Washington, D.C.: Government Printing Office. 17:509; 41:251.

Constitution of the United States of America, Article 1, Section 3; Article 1, Section 9, Paragraph 3; Amendment 17.

Daynes, Kathryn M. *More Wives than One: Transformation of the Mormon Marriage System, 1840–1910.* Urbana: University of Illinois Press, 2001.

De Hartog, Leo. *Genghis Khan: Conqueror of the World.* New York: Barnes & Noble Publishing, 1999.

Deseret News. 18 October 1871.

Edersheim, Alfred. *Sketches of Jewish Social Life in the Days of Christ.* Grand Rapids: Wm. B. Eerdmans Publishing Company, reprinted 1982.

Edersheim, Alfred. *The Life and Times of Jesus the Messiah.* Reprint edition. Grand Rapids: Wm. B. Eerdmans Publishing Company, reprinted 1981.

Embry, Jessie L. *Mormon Polygamous Families: Life in the Principle.* Salt Lake City: University of Utah Press, 1987.

Embry, Jessie L. *Setting the Record Straight, Mormons & Polygamy.* Orem: Millennial Press, 2007.

Farrar, Frederic. *The Life of Christ.* 2 vols. New York: E.P. Dutton & Company, 1874.

Firmage, Edwin Brown and Richard Collin Mangrum. *Zion In The Courts: A Legal History of the Church of Jesus Christ of Latter-day Saints 1830–1900.* Urbana and Chicago: University of Illinois Press, 1988.

Geikie, Cummingham. *The Life and Words of Christ.* Revised ed., 2 vols. New York: Appleton & Company, 1891, 1894.

History of the Church of Jesus Christ of Latter Day Saints. 4th ed. 4 vols. Independence: Board of Publication of the Reorganized Church of Jesus Christ of Latter Day Saints, 1911.

Howick, E. Keith. *The Second Coming of Jesus the Messiah.* St. George: WindRiver Publishing, 2003.

Idaho Constitution, Article I, Paragraph 4.

Jensen, Andrew. *LDS Biographical Encyclopedia.* 4 vols. Draper: Greg Kofford Books. 2005.

Johnson, Donald B. *National Party Platforms: Volume I, 1840–1956.* Champaign: University of Illinois Press, 1966.

Johnson, Donald Bruce (ed). *National Party Platforms: Volume I 1840–1856.* Urbana and Chicago: University of Illinois Press, 1978.

Johnson, Jeffrey O. "Determining and Defining 'Wife': The Brigham Young Households." *Dialogue: A Journal of Mormon Thought* 20:3 (1987): 62–63.

Kimball, Spencer W. *Faith Precedes the Miracle.* Salt Lake City: Deseret Book, 1972.

Kimball, Spencer W. *The Miracle of Forgiveness.* Salt Lake City: Bookcraft, 1969.

Larson, Gustave O. *The "Americanization" of Utah for Statehood.* San Marion: The Huntington Library, 1971.

Linn, William Alexander. *The Story Of The Mormons From The Date Of Origin To The Year 1901.* New

York: The MacMillan Company; London: Macmillan & Co., Ltd., 1902.

Manson, Pamela. "Utah Trio Challenges State Laws Banning Polygamy," *The Salt Lake Tribune* 13 January 2004, sec. C:6.

McCormick, John S. *Salt Lake City, The Gathering Place: An Illustrated History.* Salt Lake City: Signature Books, 1980.

Messenger and Advocate. 15 March 1845. 1:176.

Millennial Star. Manchester, England. Vol 3:74.

New Mexico Constitution, Article XXI, Paragraph 1.

Oklahoma Constitution, Article I, Paragraph 2.

"Polygamy 'Stronghold' Raided, Arizona police Nab 346." *Oakland Tribune,* 27 July 1953.

Prospectus of the *Nauvoo Expositor.* 7 June 1844.

Quote from the *Boston Bee. Times and Seasons.* 15 March 1843: Vol. IV, No. 9: 143.

Renard, John. *Responses to 101 Questions on Hinduism.* Mawah: Paulist Press. March 1999.

Richardson, James D. *A Compilation of the Messages and Papers of the Presidents, 1789–1897.* Fourth State of the Union Address. Washington, D.C.: Government Printing Office, 1896–99.

Roberts, B. H. *Comprehensive History of the Church of Jesus Christ of Latter-day Saints.* 6 vols. Salt Lake City: Deseret Book Company, 1930.

"Salt Lake City." *Utah History Encyclopedia.* Salt Lake City: University of Utah Press, 1994.

Senate Document 486. Senate Committee on Privileges and Elections. "In the Matter of the Protests Against the Right of Hon. Reed Smoot, A Senator from the State of Utah to Hold His Seat." 59th Congress. First Session. Vol. 4932. Washington: General Printing Office, 1970.

Shin, Ian. "'Scoot—Smoot—Scoot': The Seating Trial of Senator Reed Smoot." *Gains Junction Undergraduate*

Interdisciplinary Journal of History. College Station: Texas A & M University, Spring 2005.

"Should Canada Decriminalize Polygamy and Plural Unions?" *Polygamy in Canada: Legal and Social Implications for Women and Children—A Collection of Policy Research Reports,* Status of Women Canada (Ottawa, Ontario, Canada).

Smith, Hyrum. *Times and Seasons.* John Taylor, Ed. 15 March 1844: Vol V, No. 6: 474.

Smith, Joseph F., Jr., and Richard C. Evans. *Blood Atonement and the Origin of Plural Marriage.* Salt Lake City: *Deseret News* Press, 1905.

Smith, Joseph Fielding. *Blood Atonement and the Origin of Plural Marriage.* Salt Lake City: *Deseret News* Press, n/d.

Smith, Joseph, Jr. *History of The Church of Jesus Christ of Latter-day Saints,* ed. B.H. Roberts. 7 vols. Salt Lake City: The Church of Jesus Christ of Latter-day Saints, 1955.

Smith, Joseph, Ed. *The Prophet.* 24 May 1845.

Soukup, Elise. "Polygamists, Unite!" *Newsweek* 20 May 2006.

Talmage, James E. *Jesus the Christ.* Salt Lake City: Deseret Book, 1959.

Taylor, Samuel W. *Family Kingdom.* London: Hodder and Stroughton, 1951.

The Book of Mormon. Translated by Joseph Smith, Jr. Salt Lake City: The Church of Jesus Christ of Latter-day Saints, 1981.

The Doctrine and Covenants of the Church of Jesus Christ of Latter-day Saints. Salt Lake City: The Church of Jesus of Christ of Latter-day Saints, 1981.

The Holy Bible, Containing the Old and New Testaments. Authorized King James version. Salt Lake City: The Church of Jesus Christ of Latter-day Saints, 1989.

The Pearl of Great Price. Salt Lake City: The Church of Jesus Christ of Latter-day Saints, 1981.

The Vanier Institute of the Family website: www.VIFamily.ca.

Times and Seasons. 1 September 1842: Vol. III, No. 21: 909–910.

Trench, Richard Chenevix. *Notes on the Parables of Our Lord.* Reprint ed. Grand Rapids: Baker Book House, 1965.

Turley, Jonathan. "Polygamy Laws Expose Our Own Hypocrisy." *USA Today,* 3 October 2004.

United States Statutes at Large.

Utah Constitution, Article III.

"Utah's Drive on Polygamy is Continued." *Nevada State Journal.* 12 December 1943.

Wu, Fatima. "From a Dead End to a New Road of Life: Xiao Sa's Abandoned Women." *World Literature Today,* 1991.

Young, Brigham, et al. *Journal of Discourses.* Liverpool: F.D. Richards, Latter-day Saints' Book Depot, 1855–1886.

Young, Brigham. *Deseret Evening News.* Salt Lake City, Utah. 14 November 1855.

Young, Kimball. *Isn't One Wife Enough?* New York: Henry Holt & Co., 1954.

Legal Cases Cited

Bronson v. Swenson, Case No. 2:04-CV-21 TS, U.S. District Court, District of Utah, (February 15, 2005).

Davis v. Beason, 133 U.S. 333, 346–347 (1890).

Gonzales, Attorney General, et al. v. O Centro Espirita Beneficente Uniao Dovegetal et al., No. 04-1084. (125 S. Ct. 1846) (U.S. April 18, 2005).

Lawrence et al. v. Texas, 539 US 558 (2003).

Mormon Church v. United States, Late Corporation of the Church of Jesus Christ of Latter-day Saints, et al. v. United States, Romney v. Same, 136 U.S. 1 (1890).

Reynolds v. United States, 98 U.S. 145 (1878)
Romer, Governor of Colorado, et al. v. Evans et al., 517
    U.S. 620, (1996).
Shepp v. Shepp, 821 A. 2d 635 (Pennsylvania 2006).
State of Utah v. Warren Steed Jeffs, Third District Court,
    State of Utah, Case No. 1061500526.
State v. Green, 99 P.3D 820 (Utah 2004).
State v. Holm, 137 P.3d 726 (Utah 2006).
Wisconsin v. Yoder, 406 U.S. 205, 213 (1972).

Federal Acts Cited

Edmunds Act, Statutes 22:30 (1882).
Edmunds-Tucker Act, Statutes 24:635 (1887).
Morrill Anti-bigamy Act, Statutes 12:501 (1862).
Poland Act, Statutes 18:253 (1874).

Index _____

revelation first appeared in 1876 edition of, 20; priesthood meeting approves publication of, 25; Section 132 interpreted, 48; standard work of LDS Church, 2.

Edmonds Act, 86; accomplishments of, 87; church leaders go underground after passage, 88; imposed civil punishments on entire Mormon community, 88; offered to Congress as means of punishing Mormons, 88; replaces bigamy with polygamy as crime, 87.

Edmonds-Tucker Act, 89; attempt to take absolute political control of Utah Territory, 91; constitutionality of affirmed, 92 designed to dismantle LDS Church, 91; prosecutions under became persecution, 92; sixteen accomplishments of, 89.

Emigration, President Cleveland urges Congress to stop all into country, 91.

End, Ends, Ending, all contracts not made to this end have end when men are dead, 51; they shall be gods because they have no end, 55.

Endow, Endowment, those called by the Father, as Aaron, are endowed with keys of priesthood, 65.

Enigma, definition, viii.

Enlarge, angels did not abide law, so could not be enlarged, 53.

Enter, no one can reject covenant and enter into the Lord's glory, 50.

Escape, the Lord will make way for saints' escape, 63.

Eternal Life, this is eternal lives — to know the only wise and true God, 56; Joseph Smith to be given crowns of eternal lives in eternal worlds, 64.

Eternal, Eternally, that which elders bind on earth shall be eternally bound in heavens, 61.

Eternity, anointed both for time and for all eternity, 53, 54.

Everlasting, Everlastingly, they shall be gods from everlasting to everlasting, 55.

Exaltation, denied if commit murder, 57; requirements of defined, 57; ministering angels remain without exaltation, 53; Abraham, Isaac and Jacob have entered into their exaltation, 59; the Lord seals upon Joseph Smith his exaltation, 62.

Facts, concerning polygamy during Joseph Smith era, 6.

Faithful, Faithfulness, wife of adulterer to be given unto him who has been faithful, 60.

Family, can last beyond earth life, 51.

Fear, reason for denials of polygamy, 36.

Few, few find the way that leads to exaltation, 56.

Find, Found, find narrow way to exaltation, 56.

Forgive, Forgiven, Forgiveness, blasphemy against Holy Ghost shall not be forgiven, 56.

Fruit, Fruitful, Abraham received promises concerning fruit of his loins, 58.

Fulness, everlasting covenant instituted for fulness of the Lord's glory, 50.

Garden of Eden, marriage instituted in, 12.

Gate, strait is gate to exaltation, 56; broad is gate to the deaths, 56.

Glory, Glorify, new and everlasting covenant instituted for fulness of glory, 54, 55; glory is fulness and continuation of seeds forever, 54; work of Father continues that he may be glorified, 66.

God, commanded Abraham to receive Hagar, 58; man can become themselves, 55; no man shall come to Father but by Christ, 52.

Gods, angels who do not abide law become not gods, but angels of God, 53; if marriage sealed by Holy Spirit of promise, they can pass the gods appointed, 53, 54; those who receive exaltation are gods and have no end, 55, 59; Abraham, Isaac, and Jacob are gods, not angels, 59.

Gonzales v. O Centro, case, 131; expanded religious freedom rights, 132; may be chink in Reynolds case, 132.

Great Salt Lake Valley, growth of, 46.

Hagar, given to Abraham, 58, 66; God commanded Abraham to marry, 58.

Hale, Emma, see Smith, Emma Hale.

Hand, will I receive at your hands that which I have not appointed, 52.

Handmaid, Emma Smith is addressed as handmaid, 63.

Hayes, Rutherford B., tells Congress to take away power of the church, 73.

Head, exaltation sealed upon heads of those whose marriage is sealed by Holy Spirit of promise, 54.

Holy Ghost, blasphemy against Holy Ghost, 56; marriage must be sealed by to continue beyond earth life, 51; individuals will be ministering angels if not sealed by, 53.

Holy Spirit of Promise, all covenants and performances must be sealed by Holy Spirit of promise to have force after this life, 53, 54, 56.

House, house of the Lord is house of order, 53.

Ignorance, listed as reason for denials of polygamy, 32.

Inherit, Inheritance, those who marry in new and everlasting covenant will inherit thrones, kingdoms, 54; David will not inherit his wives and concubines, 59.

Innumerable, Abraham's seed to continue innumerable as stars, 58.

Instruction, Instruct, obey instructions given by the Lord, 50.

Isaac, Abraham commanded to offer Isaac, 59; denies Rebekah is wife, 9; Isaac abode in God's law, 59

Jacob, the Lord justified Jacob in having many wives and concubines, 50, 59.

Jeffs, Warren Steed, arrested, xiii; convicted of two counts of assisted rape, 137; prophet of Fundamentalist Church of Jesus Christ of Latter Day Saints (FLDS), 136; Utah polygamy case of, 136.

Jesus Christ, confirms marriage relationship, 12; declares He is delivering revelation on plurality of wives, 56; to have eternal lives is to know God and Jesus Christ, 56.

Jews, living polygamy in New Testament times, 14.

Key, only one holds keys at a time, 51; man holding keys of power should teach wife law of priesthood, 66.

Kimball, Heber C., states would be damned if oppose plurality of wives, 43.

Kingdom, those married by new and everlasting covenant inherit kingdoms, principalities, 54.

Kingsley, Joseph C., makes a copy of the polygamy revelation, 19; testifies that Joseph had multiple wives, 20.

Know, Knew, few find way to exaltation because they do not know the Lord, 56; eternal lives is to know the only wise and true God, 56.

Lamech, first recorded Biblical polygamist, 13, 159.

Last Days, Joseph Smith appointed to hold power in last days, 51.

Law of Moses, concubines regulated under, 13 ftnt; polygamy continued under, 13.

Law, the Lord's word is his law, 52; except ye abide my law, ye cannot attain celestial glory, 55; those who enter into the Lord's law shall be saved, 58.

Lawrence v. Texas, case, 130; involved homosexuality, 130; may affect Reynolds case, 130.

Lectures on Faith, contained in first Doctrine & Covenants, 26.

Life, Lives, strait is gate that leads unto continuation of the lives, 56.

Lincoln, Abraham, homily to leave Brigham Young alone, 74.

Loins, Abraham received promises concerning the fruit of his loins, 58.

Lyon, Aaron, claimed to receive revelation that Sister Jackson should be wife, 20.

Magnify, the Lord will magnify his name, 66.

Man, can become gods, 55; can still be sealed to

multiple women under certain conditions, 149; requirements of under the law of plurality of wives, 67.

Manifesto of 1890, 97; advised members to obey law of the land, 99; did not deal with problem of cohabitation, 109; did not destroy belief in plurality of wives, 104; did not restrict practice of polygamy, 106; does not renounce polygamy, 102; explained, 100–104; Lorin C. Woolley claimed authority to continue polygamy after, 124; Official Declaration—1, 97; polygamy practiced after, 6; sustained at general conference of church, 100.

Manifesto of 1904, 105; did not deal with problem of cohabitation, 109; Joseph F. Smith issued, 106; sustained in general conference of church, 108.

Marriage, Article on, 26; can exist beyond earth life, 51; Congress moved to define, 143; Edmunds-Tucker Act requires public record of all, 90; instituted in Garden of Eden, 12; ministering angels if not sealed by Holy Ghost, 53; must be performed by proper authority, 51; polygamist limits of defined, 60; polygamist marriages must be authorized by prophet, 54; polygamy a form of, 13; polygamy revelation named celestial, 20; properly sealed can procreate after earth life, 55; testimonies of obedience to by early authorities, 41; will states change definition of, 132.

Marriage, Marry, if man and woman marry in world, it is of no force when they are out of world, 53; those out of world neither marry nor are given in marriage, 53; marriage by new and everlasting covenant leads to exaltation, 54, 55; order of plural marriage not adultery, 65.

McKean, James B., appointed federal judge in Utah Territory, 77; indicts Brigham Young for lewd and lascivious relations, 78; rabidly anti-Mormon, 77.

Mexico, polygamy continued in after Manifesto, 106; polygamy illegal in, 7.

Ministering Angels, serve as if marriage not sealed by Holy Ghost, 53.

Morality, not expected of people in Utah Territory, 77.

Mormon Church, see Church of Jesus Christ of Latter-day Saints.

Morrill Anti-bigamy Act, 74; accomplishments of, 75; classifies polygamy as bigamy, 75; problems of enforcing, 79; prohibited charitable organization from holding property valued in excess of $50,000, 76; revoked church Incorporation Act, 75; test case to determine constitutionality of, 84.

Included in this index are the index keys and references found in The Doctrine and Covenants *Index for Section 132 as published by The Church of Jesus Christ of Latter-day Saints.*